Voices From The Pandemic

Edited by Don Helin

Compiled by Headline Books

Headline Books, Inc.
Terra Alta, WV

Voices From The Pandemic

Edited by Don Helin

To order additional copies of this book or for book publishing information,

Headline Books, Inc.
P.O. Box 52
Terra Alta, WV 26764

www.HeadlineBooks.com
Tel: 304-789-3001

Email: mybook@headlinebooks.com

ISBN 13: 9781951556433

Library of Congress Control Number: 2020945459

PRINTED IN THE UNITED STATES OF AMERICA

Dedication

Our Anthology is dedicated to the millions of heroes who kept us alive and safe during this fearful time: healthcare workers, police and fire, EMT's, over-the-road truckers, grocery clerks, public transit workers, and so many others. ***Thank You All.***

Contents

Introduction

A memoir is a journey through the writer's past. It is not an autobiography – one's entire life – but a slice of life.

The trying period since January 1, 2020 makes sense to each of us because we have lived through it. Our readers, on the other hand, need to make sense of the changes during the period covered by our memoir. The task for us as writers is not only to tell the reader what happened during the Coronovirus period, but to bring them along on the journey so they can experience it for themselves.

The last six months is similar to a number of other critical times in our history — the Kennedy assassination, the landing on the moon, and the 911 attack. Everyone remembers where they were during those times and undoubtedly they will remember what they were doing during the Coronovirus Pandemic. Having written a memoir of your experience will help others understand what you did during this trying period.

Creative nonfiction is useful in a memoir as it helps bring scenes alive with enhanced setting and dialogue. Many personal history memoirs succeed because the writer transforms real people into compelling, fleshed-out characters on the page.

In May 2020, a number of people attended **Zoom Into Books** workshops provided on the story-telling techniques needed to help document a 'new normal' memoir. Headline Books posted a call for submissions and the response was overwhelming.

We have tried to capture voices from the Pandemic — **healthcare workers, educators, people who have experienced loss, writers and entertainers without audiences, and a special group, sixth graders** trying to understand, why? None of these voices know what the future holds. We don't either, but we have tried to document where we are now.

We hope you enjoy the stories in this anthology and perhaps better understand what this trying period has meant to so many of us.

Don Helin, Editor *Cathy Teets, Publisher*

Ouroboros

by Robert E. Furey

Field studies classes are designed for changing people's worldviews. Seeing different horizons prepares one for change, a desirable trait for any learner to develop. With that in mind, my students and I put together a spring break class to the Great American South West. We left one world for Utah and Colorado in the second week of March 2020. We returned to another.

Of course, we'd heard a monster slouched into the awareness of our lives. They told us it was coming. A far off city named Wuhan with something called a "wet market" had summoned up a boogeyman, liberating it on all of us. But why fall for one more cataclysm? Yet another Mayan calendar ticking up to the end of days. Armageddon, Ragnarök, Gotterdammerung, Doomsday: just another implacable reckoning that came like a screaming banshee and passed as a zephyr in the night. An end of days our small band refused to acknowledge. How could we? After so many threats deflated, we scoffed, and we laughed.

For a week, our home in Utah would be a 27-foot recreational vehicle boasting seven berths. It's odd to think that such a short time ago, so many of us were comfortable in such a small space. Eating, sleeping, laughing, all in that tiny shared space that in slightly different circumstances would have been difficult for even a single person. For us, we only held eagerness for the coming days and the broad circuit we would make through Utah and Colorado's rocks and sands.

We crossed the mountains from Utah for Dinosaur, Colorado, at night. Through a maelstrom of whiteout conditions, slashing horizontal snow, and chains of cliff-edged switchbacks, the RV made slow progress. A headlong rush through the mountains risked precipice and tumble into a deeper black. We knew to stop, but to be honest, we pressed on, through the storm, when we should have found a place to sleep long before we did.

We covered most of the trail and had but few miles left before Dinosaur in the morning. In hindsight, it was the hike up the mountain to visit the "Wall of Bones" that Joey first started showing signs. He was dragging, stopping more and more frequently. By the time we reached the Dinosaur Quarry building at the top, his forehead dripped with sweat. None of us noticed, at least none of us said. Joey himself might have dismissed it as just a bad day. He told us he was tired.

Inside the Dinosaur Quarry building, the Triassic and Jurassic fossil beds built up the "Wall of Bones." Dinosaur remains etched the stone with the runes of a world 145 million years gone in an extinction event of largely unknown cause. But the world altered and erased so many dream creatures, like stegosaurids and the iconic long-necked sauropods. Changes so long-ago, ideas of good and bad had not applied. Now, of course, an event we can confidently call bad for dinosaurs, good for people.

It's impossible to catalog all the catastrophes and threats of catastrophe through time. Often we are left with nothing more than rubble and mystery, a gaping hole where sense and explanation might have been. Then they fade, lessons dissipated and dispersed through Brownian motion and time.

The western edge of Colorado stretches with mountain vistas. Our trek from Dinosaur to Mesa Verde overlooked so many rocky mountain peaks and valleys it seemed the petrified surface of a churning sea. From the back of the RV, Katy and Alexi started singing "America the Beautiful" in what became the most haunting moments of the trip. Their voices, gentle and sweet, seemed to drift over the crags' innocence and power. It is my memory of "then" and juxtaposed sharply against the new world of "now."

Joey was dragging at Mesa Verde. Hot and dry, we all felt it.

But Joey's skin had grown crimson. His features pained even on limited walks, so much so it had grown too difficult to ignore. I took him aside and asked him how he was feeling."

"I'm just tired, Doc," he said. "I'm not sleeping well."

I gazed at him a moment, and then a moment more. And I could see it. "How long have you been feeling sick?" I paused, but before he could respond, I continued. "And don't bother lying to me."

His hesitating response stuttered off the Band-Aid. "About a week. Maybe more."

I didn't know what to do. With most of the week left to go, suddenly the specter of something bad appeared among us. I couldn't send him home, and at that point, what good would it have done? I couldn't leave him in a motel. There remained no legitimate options.

The Cliff Palace at Mesa Verda was abandoned by 1300 AD. Standing on the ledge overlooking the Puebloan structures built into the cliffside, it was hard to imagine the building noisy with community. It was hard to see why they settled there in the first place. But they had, and they stayed for almost 1000 years under very harsh conditions.

Some extinctions are so close to home we feel them. An abandoned city is unlikely ever to promote good thoughts. Where did they go? Why did they go? What brought about this change? While there are theories concerning Cliff Palace's demise, we ultimately have a mystery along the lines of Jurassic extinction. Only now it's people, now it's bad.

Once returned to the RV, Joey was exiled to the rear sleeping area. Once outed, Joey slept only waking to eat and drink. I'm not sure what good it did. In a 27 foot RV without partitions, whatever he had, we all had been exposed to it already. No one seemed outwardly concerned unless spoken of directly. Otherwise, superstition required we not mention the monster by name.

Zigzagging across the map, we found our way to Promontory, Utah. On May 10, 1869, the Golden Spike was driven in to complete the connection between the Central Pacific and Union Pacific Railroads. Not all changes were bad ones. This one changed the world from the small to the large, from ease of sending a letter to arteries of trade goods from all over the planet. Driving the spike might even be the seminal moment when the United States went from another regional government to a world power. Whatever the changes before and after Leland Stanford swung that spike maul, the world had changed forever.

In some respects, we might look at the time leading up to COVID as our own moment of change. Mankind has faced pandemics before, with horrendous death tolls, but who really remembers them? Sure, we know numbers, can call up spreadsheets of the dead. But who among us groks, the wailing of those realizing death stalked them, or the chasms left after so many had gone?

A few days later, Joey was up and back with the rest of us. His angry flush had faded to quiet recovery, whatever plagued him in retreat. I paid empty diligence to watch for signs in myself and the students. I admit an expectation to see the monster's head again.

Our meandering through the Southwest was closing with a pass through the Arches, spectacular geological formations. When portions of the southwest were left as dry sea beds 65 million years ago and lifted high through tectonic forces, sedimentary sandstone was geologically torqued to new high deserts. The humps and rolling ridgeways sculpted by eddies of wind and water into Daliesque archways, like bridges, one after another. This constant blooming and collapse of arches in space and time left behind a landscape in flux only "observable" through scattered rubble mounds, themselves ever whittled by sand and rain.

Just days after our return, the world capsized. We met in class just two days before the university was summarily shut down with just three days allotted for building an online curriculum to complete the semester. That was 120 days ago as I write this missive. One hundred and twenty days of lockdown, the post-COVID 19 side of reality shift, a golden spike, before and after layers of dinosaur bones, an arch carved in geological time that fell in a moment of random weather, an abandoned city.

As for us, we traded seven days of isolation and freedom for a new flavor, isolation and lockdown, 120 days and no end in sight. All of us fell sick in the week shortly after our return. There was no readily available COVID-19 testing that early, so what we had remains a mystery. But given the rapidity of the general collapse, we lived the fear of hosting the virus.

The great difficulty now remains how to rebuild. Unfortunately, even here in the midst of it, we don't know what this new world really looks like yet, only what we left behind. One thing is certain; the future will remember us. Whatever stories we tell now, fates willing, might help the next time. But my bet's on forgetting until another round.

Rob Furey *is a professor of integrative science at Harrisburg University. He regularly takes his students on field experiences in Brazil, Puerto Rico, the Everglades, and the Chesapeake Bay. The included story depicts his first expedition to Utah with students. Rob is also a science writer and a science fiction author, and has a few too many pets.*

The Tidal Wave

by Marie McGowan

The low rumble of warning that would become the tidal wave of Covid-19 began in late December or early January with the reports of an illness out of Wuhan, China. At the time, both healthcare and I did not realize how this seismic event would profoundly change how we practice both in the short term and long term.

I have been practicing physical therapy (PT) for 32 years in many different areas of health care but have never been considered a front-line provider. As physical therapists (PT's), occupational therapists (OT's) and speech therapists (SLP's), rehab providers are tasked not with saving lives, but are second-line healthcare providers who work with patients to maximize function and wellness. I often liken us to the "coaches" or "trainers" of health care. We are highly trained professionals who care deeply about our patient's health outcomes. I personally have been working with cancer patients for the last 20 years to minimize the complications – fatigue, neuropathy, lymphedema, scar tissue restrictions, joint stiffness, etc. – of the lifesaving treatments that they are given. It is rewarding work that brings me joy

So, I followed the news out of China and the WHO with interest, and maybe some curiosity, but not initial alarm. Cancellation of the Chinese New Year, lock downs in Wuhan, outbreak on the Diamond Princess, Italian hospitals overwhelmed. None of these events in and of itself concerning to my day to day life. The second week of March, however, the initial water and waves started to reach my life. Outbreak at a nursing home in Kirkland, Washington, frantic calls from my daughter, Heather, and daughter-in-law, Taylor, in Chicago about what to do to stay safe, the nursing home where my son, Patrick, works shuttering its doors to visitors, Rita Wilson and TOM HANKS testing positive in Australia, NBA and March Madness cancelled.

During this period, the hospital system where I work was developing its strategies for dealing with the expected influx of Covid patients. They created new positions for working on the Covid floors and for managing the entrances as visitors were being asked not to come to the hospitals and clinics. Entry managers would screen anyone coming into the facility, pass out masks and take temperatures. I dubbed this position "the Bouncer." Site Managers would be assigned to patients who were diagnosed with Covid or being tested for Covid to log everyone in/out of the room, observe donning and doffing of PPE, making sure supplies were available, passing equipment, laundry, lab samples, and medications in and out of rooms, and making sure that everyone was following the rules designed to keep everyone safe. I dubbed this position "the Hall Monitor."

Then patients started cancelling in massive numbers and we had skeletal looking schedules. Referrals were not being made to the clinic, elective surgeries were cancelled, and of all things, screening mammograms were put on hold. So, in healthcare, we live and die (no pun intended) by the numbers and would not be able to stay open at full staffing with the situation as it was.

I ordered new scrubs, set up a "decontamination station" just off my garage, and set off for my first week of shifts. 12 hours is way different from 8 hours. Overnights are a totally different rhythm. The first day I was there, I was assigned to ICU to a ventilator patient. The nurses were kind and answered all of my stupid questions and put up with a new person on their unit who did not know where anything was. I was really in over my head. I didn't know what a saline flush, green cap, or coupling device looked like. *Was this alarm important? Did the nurse need to go back in, or could she just silence it?* The procedures for Site Managers changed weekly, then daily, then what seemed like hourly.

The last shift of my first week, I was a floater. I was trying to find my way around a hospital that I was not familiar with to check on each of the units and relieve staff for bathroom or meal breaks. I ended up several times outside of the OR, the psych unit, and wandering labyrinthine halls. Early that afternoon, I was checking the unit where I had worked the day earlier. There was no Site Manager outside of the rooms. The nurse for the rooms was nearly in tears and the nurse manager for the unit told me she had sent the Site Manager home. She was not paying attention to the nurse who was well into her third 12-hour shift as she was donning her PPE and the nurse nearly went in without a face shield. The nurses in that position are tired by that time and their mind is on providing care for the patient. They were being asked to "cluster" care – take everything in for that session that they need – to preserve PPE. They are depending on the Site Managers to make sure they are safe, and the Site Manager broke her trust with that nurse. That hammered home to me how important the position was.

I ended up working in the position for 3 months, before I was able to resume my prior position. I worked with great nurses and good and not so good Site Managers. There was a rhythm to the days and weeks. Many hours of boredom fractured by moments of sheer terror. The parts of the job that wore on me the most were the alarms, the quick and constant decision making, and the suffering and death. There is a reason that I am a PT. I like developing relationships with people over time, solving problems with them jointly, and the deliberate, thoughtful decision making that are parts of my job. What was required here was moving on to the next patient, fixing the problem of the moment, and quick problem solving. I very often did not know what happened to a patient after they left my unit.

I used yoga, journaling, and meditation to deal with the situation, but the stress eventually creeped in. I began to develop heartburn which I had not had previously. I also started experiencing severe anxiety and panic attacks.

I was not prepared to see prisoners, nursing home residents, and fellow employees, suffer and die from the disease. I saw during my time a woman writhing on the floor, ripping her clothes off as she was coming down off of heroin, a woman, whose 21-year-old son found her and revived her, her brain fried and body in constant seizures, a woman who found her brother dead of Covid now hospitalized from the same disease, the eyes of a man whose heart stopped in the CT scanner, and a man, who waved and smiled at me as he was wheeled into the hospital, die weeks later on a ventilator. The person who stuck with the most to me was a sweet lady with dementia with who came in the first day of one of my weeks, scared and hollering. She turned 85 years old the last day of my week. The nurses got flowers, a card for her, and sang "Happy Birthday." She waved at me through the glass and beckoned me to come in all day. I waved back and talked to her through the glass. As the day went on, it became apparent that she was having more difficulty breathing and her oxygen levels were dropping precipitously. The doctor and nurses were desperately trying to find her family/next of kin to get a decision about intubating her. They had not reached anyone by the time my shift was over and I never saw her again. I know logically that it is not my responsibility, but I was witness to a part of their stories and feel that I need to keep them sacred.

I saw the death of too many people to count. It was not a "good" death either. Family was allowed to come in for one hour at the end of life. Sometimes we were praying for them to get there in time. We had to assist them with donning and doffing PPE while trying to give them the privacy to say goodbye. Pastors talked to and prayed with family through glass doors on walkie talkies. I saw husbands and wives die within days of each other. I saw patients make the decision not to be intubated then when the oxygen hunger started change their minds out of fear. The outcome was not any different, it just happened 3 or 5 days later.

I was in charge of the process of making sure the body was properly cared for and sent to the morgue. I had to wipe down the body bags and stretcher when the gurney was wheeled out of the room. I felt the fading warmth and firmness of the flesh beneath the plastic of the biohazard bag. I definitely did not sign up for this and was not in any way prepared to experience this. This was the destruction caused by the tidal wave of the virus.

I have returned to my clinic and am now at full schedule again, finally. The waters are receding, but it has not been without lasting results both personally and professionally.

I cannot do my job without being in close proximity to people. The American Physical Therapy Association recently released a statement about PPE for therapists, I guess some therapists are not to be provided with adequate equipment. Following the newest science, activities like mobilizing a patient (transferring, walking, exercising), adjusting ventilator or trach equipment, and causing them to breathe deeply will aerosolize viral particles into the air. This puts the practitioner at greater risk for breathing in the particles. Why are we also not talking about gyms where these activities take place? Just distance will not mitigate the risk in these places. We all need adequate PPE to keep us safe. I recently read an article about the PT for a college rowing team infecting the whole team, so I guess that the danger goes both ways.

The panic attacks and anxiety have mostly receded, but I am taking medicine now and working with a counselor. The heartburn, I fear, is here for some time and again, I am taking medicine. The therapist, who was also a full time Site Manager, and I have never been the best of friends, but when she came back to the clinic, she sought me out. She wanted to know about my experiences and shared hers.

I have lived mostly in my own bubble with Michael. He was a huge support to me as he always is. He would feed me, put me to bed, stand me up the next morning (or night) for the next shift, offer a shoulder for support or crying, encourage me, and make me laugh. He is the yin to my yang. I have Zoom happy hour with the family and have talked almost daily with some member of my family. I feel closer to Heather than I ever have. It has allowed us the time to work through our differences and distill what is important in life. Pandemics have a way of doing that. Silver linings and rainbows during the storm also exist.

Marie McGowan *has practiced physical therapy for the past 32 years, spending the last 20 years working with cancer and lymphedema patients. She is also a daughter, wife, mother, and friend. She loves outdoor activities, music, reading, and anything creative.*

When the Music Stopped

by Joe Coleman

We all heard the whispers… there was a mysterious virus out there that was going to devastate the world. It was something mentioned on cable television, almost casually, at first. It didn't have a name. It hadn't been confirmed to be true, but it was floating around in the air, something very dangerous that was more than a possibility. More like an inevitability, but we can't be sure. None of us took it too seriously, as we continued to go about living our lives.

Then, in mid-February, it became a reality. There were numerous cases in Wuhan, China, and people were dying. Worse, no one seemed to know what it was or what to do about it. But, it was "over there," so, no need to fear. It's something "they" need to deal with and get under control. This isn't something we need to deal with right now. And so, we didn't. We downplayed it. "It will go away on its own," they said.

That's pretty much how it was for me too. Just like most people, it wasn't something I focused on or understood. There was no sense that it would have any great effect on my life or that of those I love so, let's keep dancing.

It is now mid-July, and Covid 19 has impacted my life in so many ways that I can't begin to count them. But, to fully understand how I've been impacted, I should take you back to the beginning of the Pandemic and work my way forward.

On January 1st, my management team and I were busy planning my vocal group's trip to Tampa for a week of shows at Busch Gardens as part of their "Real Music, Real Legends" Series. It was an especially exciting time for us because we had a new guy in the group, Theo Peoples, and we considered this a "new" beginning. A fresh start with an amazing young talent, who happened to be the only vocalist in Motown History to have sung lead for, both, The Temptations and The Four Tops! Theo is a bad man and we're super excited!!

By January 7, 2020, I found myself onstage at Busch Gardens, Tampa, performing with my new group, Voices of Classic Soul (VOCS). Actually, on that date, we were called Coleman, Blunt, Peoples. You see, back in mid-September, we were faced with the unhappy task of parting ways with our longtime friend and stage mate, Glenn Leonard, who had decided to give full attention to his Glenn Leonard's Temptations Revue, which was receiving a lot of attention in the European market.

Glenn Leonard, Joe Blunt and I were members of a group called Leonard, Coleman & Blunt for over ten years. I've known these guys for most of my life. I met Joe Blunt at church at the tender age of 7 or 8 years old. Our moms were co-directors of the Junior Choir at the church and we were "automatically" in the choir. Neither of us recalls being asked if we wanted to be in the choir.

Joe met Glenn when he was 15 years old, after which he became a member of our local music circle in the DC Metro area. We performed in numerous local groups, together, before we, each, miraculously, landed with three of the most iconic groups in history. Glenn joined The Tempts, Joe B joined The Drifters, and I found my way to a 23-year career with The Platters.

With that background, let's move forward. After a very successful week of shows in Tampa, we were poised to capitalize on several opportunities that had been developing for us. We were booked for shows in Los Angeles, New York, New Jersey, Richmond, Florida, and West Virginia; had book fairs scheduled in Houston and Chicago regarding our book, *My Time to Shine* and, were scheduling recording sessions to record new material to stay "current."

In other words, things were looking up for us. We did a Valentine's Day performance, at a beautiful Supper Club, in Alexandria, VA, called The Carlyle Club. The place was packed with many of our loyal fans who came to experience the new group and the "new guy" in the group, Theo Peoples. Electricity was in the air and Theo didn't disappoint. Singing "Baby I Need Your Lovin'" at a fever pitch, he won our fans over before the first song ended!

As we head into March 2020, it is becoming increasingly clear that this coronavirus is very serious. The medical experts are sounding the alarm and advising us that this is an extremely deadly disease transmitted through the air. However, they make two critical errors in their explanation of what we're dealing with: they say, "only medical personnel" need to wear masks (at least, they weren't sure) and, they tell us the disease doesn't seem to affect young people. They say it's a disease that affects the elderly and the infirmed. The problem being, our youth embrace this "theory" fully and completely, causing them to be somewhat reckless in how they deal with the disease from a "social" perspective.

Everyone is now in a panic to get supplies and prepare for a lockdown to flatten the curve of this, now devastating, virus. My wife and I rush to the store only to find that shelves are emptying rapidly. Hand sanitizer, paper towels, Lysol, and other disinfectant-cleaning products are entirely out of stock, with toilet paper (can someone please explain this phenomenon?) being "all the rage." Yes, toilet paper is flying off the shelves and is being hoarded, as if it were made of gold!

As the days go by, I begin to hear of friends and family who have the virus. This is very scary because, due to the pandemic (yes – by now, the experts have declared Covid 19 a pandemic!), we are becoming further removed from each other. As the threat level increased, ALL personal contact is being discouraged. No handshaking, no hugs. Six feet is beginning to feel like six miles as we are asked to stay as far away from each other as possible. As a hugger, this is hard!

It is in this environment I learn that Andre Jackson, my former stage mate, with Glenn's Temptations group, has the virus. He posted it on Facebook - that's how I learn about Andre's situation. Soon after that, Pia, the mother of my Goddaughter, Imani, sends me a text message indicating she has the virus. I'm stunned! It is becoming increasingly clear this disease is "random." Andre is an entertainer and Pia is an attorney. Coronavirus does not discriminate.

By mid-April, most of the east coast, California, and several "northern" states are in complete lockdown. My wife, Vanessa, and I decide, early on, that we are sheltering in place, as mandated by the Governor. We (really I) only leave the house to go to the store for groceries and necessary items. I'm not leaving my house unless it's necessary and Vanessa isn't leaving the house period!

Sadly, as we enter the month of May, domestic violence cases skyrocket during the pandemic, as abusers are sheltered in place with their victims – usually wives and girlfriends. Covid 19 has brought one thing into focus. Vanessa and I really Like each other, AND we love each other, as well! We couldn't imagine "sheltering in place" for months with someone we didn't love and care about how we do. She has been my rock!

I'm learning a lot about myself while dealing with this coronavirus. I can make do with a lot less in terms of "stuff." I tend to procrastinate, but I'm working hard on improving my "turn-around" times. I have a great "need" to be in touch with my family – I have two sisters (Claudette and Barbara), who live in Chicago and Baltimore, respectively, and one brother – William (the recluse), who lives in Clover, VA. I check in with them regularly, just to hear their voices.

As an entertainer, the consequences and outcomes of the pandemic are coming fully into focus. We had cancellation after cancellation as far as gigs go. It was slow at first. Initially, there were "postponements" and "let's wait and sees." Then, slowly, by late-March – early-April, the cancellation notices started coming in, until I looked up one day and realized, ALL my/our gigs were gone, through the end of 2020.

There is nothing more devastating to a performer than to have nothing on the calendar for the foreseeable future. What do I do, when you can't even go out and get a "straight" gig? How do I take care of my family and keep a roof over our heads? I'm still in the process of answering these very difficult questions. Stay tuned… there is *still* a crisis in progress!

Joe Coleman *was a member of "The Platters" for 23 years and was a regular at the Sahara Hotel in Las Vegas performing popular songs such as "Only You," "My Prayer," "Smoke Gets in Your Eyes," "The Great Pretender," and many more Number One hits.*

He is co-author of the award-winning book, My Time to Shine, *a memoir of the careers of Coleman, Joe Blunt, former lead singer of The Drifters, and Glenn Leonard, former lead singer of The Temptations, with J. Michael Williard.*

Joe Coleman and Joe Blunt are Zoom Into Books Authors.

Fighting the Shadows

by Jennifer D. Diamond

The bedroom door is open enough to let soft light stream across the room. My sandbag limbs feel pinned to the mattress, my head a fifty-pound boulder. When I force my eyes to open for a second, I notice my husband's black dress shirt. The suite-shirt still hangs on the back of the closet door even though it's been weeks since he's had to wear it—since he's left the house for work. It's become a part of the landscape, a testament to our resistance, our inability to admit we're not going back to work, "back to normal," anytime soon.

The shirt, a dark outline against the light finish of the closet door, transforms into a liquid blob and slides off the hanger out of sight. My heavy eyelids close, then open with unfocused fuzziness, and the opaque shadow hovers at the foot of my bed, oozing malevolence.

A freezing wave washes from chin to toes, like the early July Atlantic Ocean breaking over my shoulders without warning on the beaches of Cape Cod. My pulse whooshes in my ears. My screams stick in my throat. I'm paralyzed. This isn't the first time I've encountered the shadows. They began appearing when I was three years old.

I slipped, didn't fall, but water splashed over the sides of the bowl I carried. I bit my tongue to hold in a little yell because I didn't want to wake anyone up on Saturday morning.

I pushed the screen door with my butt, went onto the back porch, and poured water from the bowl into the kittens' dish. I set the bowl down and kneeled. I put my forehead on the wood, hands around my eyes, trying to see between the boards, to where they slept under the porch.

I whispered, "Here, kitty-kitty-kitty."

The kittens ran up the porch steps. I opened my arms for them and counted as they crawled all over me. *Only five?* To keep track, I touched their heads; Star, Pooh, Lily, Aggie, Felix. *Where's Oscar?*

I stood up and brushed the gray paint chips off my legs. I saw him as soon as I looked through the porch railing. He was asleep on his side in the rocks beside the steps, tail straight, tongue sticking out. I wasn't allowed off the porch unless a grown-up was outside with me, but I wanted him to wake up. Back in the kitchen, I filled the same Tupperware dish I used to give the kitties a drink. This time I took the dish to the porch railing, lifted my hand over the top, and poured water onto Oscar. His orange fur smooshed flat from the wetness, but he was still sleeping. I went back to the kitchen sink, filled up again, and let the water trickle onto his head. His tongue moved, so I gave him more drinks. But Oscar was still asleep when the sun started feeling too hot on my skin, too bright in my eyes.

"What'cha doing?"

My arms flew up in the air, and I dropped the bowl. The fancy Tupperware hit the bottom stair, bounced off the rocks, and landed in the yard.

"Oh no," I ran down the stairs, into the cool grass, grabbed the bowl and ran back up to the porch.

"Give it," my big sister, Julie, said as she yanked it from my hands. I put my fists on my hips and scrunched my face at her, but this made her laugh.

"Look," she said, "you scratched it."

I ruined the Tupperware. My belly flipped and flopped. Am I going to get in trouble?

"What are you doing with it?"

My sister looked over the railing. Her breathing changed.

Her face looked scared, sad, mad, all at once. My skin tingled with goosebumps.

I followed her as she ran into the house, through the kitchen, down the hallway, to the bottom of the stairs. My head bumped into the backs of her legs when she stopped.

"Dad," she yelled, "we need you."

"What?" The closed bedroom door muffled his voice.

"On the back porch."

Julie was going to tattle on me. I was in big trouble.

"What?" He stood at the top of the stairs wearing only his white underwear.

"Out back," my sister said.

She spun me around and grabbed my shoulders. I tried to duck away from her, but she forced me to walk. I didn't want to go back that way. I spilled water all over the kitchen floor and scratched the good Tupperware. I went off the porch without a grown-up. I was bad.

On the porch again, Julie pointed toward Oscar.

"Down there," she said.

Her hands felt hot and heavy on my shoulders. My dad ran down the stairs. I knew this was serious because he was outside in his underwear. He said a curse word in a soft voice.

"Did he wake up?" I asked.

Julie squeezed my shoulders.

"No, Honey."

"Why?" I asked.

He put one knee on the porch, but his face was still higher than mine. He looked down at me, his eyes red and watery.

"He's dead, Honey."

"Why?"

"Probably a Tom," he said to my sister.

I didn't know what he was saying. Who's Tom?

He put his hands on top of my sister's hands, which were still on top of my shoulders. Hot stuff splashed up into the back of my mouth. I looked down, pushing my toe onto a splinter in the wood. The pain in my toe helped take away the burning in my throat.

Julie's hands shook my shoulders. I turned my head to look at her. Her face was red, long pieces of her blonde hair stuck to her wet cheeks, and her whole body shook. I looked at my dad. My face felt hot. My eyes were blurry. This was sad, but I didn't know *why*.

"I tried to wake him up," I said.

My words felt like hiccups. I wanted to ask if I did good, if it was a bad thing to pour water on Oscar, but it felt like I would throw up if I tried to talk again.

"We need to bury him," he said to my sister.

They went inside. I crossed my arms and put my hands on the cooling spot where my sister's hands had been on my shoulders. I sneaked a peek at Oscar, then ran inside to get away from feeling like ants were crawling all over me.

That summer, when I was three years old, a shadow in the shape of a kitten started pacing the windowsill in my bedroom. I loved Oscar, but this shadow filled me with ice. I prayed, "Now I lay me down to sleep," repeatedly until I fell asleep.

The shadows have appeared to me throughout my life during times of stress. Not in the shape of a cat, but of opaque outlines peeking their heads through doorways, lurking around the footboard of my bed, or threatening to suffocate me while I lie paralyzed, fighting to move, fighting to scream. During this time of the COVID-19 virus outbreak, my shadows have returned.

Still frozen in my bed, hot tears wet my pillow while the shadow continues to hover. Lifting to the surface of consciousness, I remind myself the shadows aren't real. They are a manifestation of a neurological pattern I inherited from my father called night terrors with sleep paralysis.

I'm dreaming. It's only a dream.

Fighting won't make the shadows disappear because they're a product of the synapses in my brain misfiring while bathed in stress hormones. Resisting stress doesn't cause stress to go away.

The opposite is true. Instead, I slow my breathing, softening into each breath, slowing my heart rate. Invoking the innocence of my three-year-old self, I recite a prayer over and over, until the shadow fades away, and I fall back to sleep.

I've taken comfort in the phrase "alone together" during this time of self-quarantine and lock-downs. Maybe your stress responses are like mine. I imagine Dr. Freud would analyze my nightmares as projections of my fear of death. Fearing death is human.

Fighting the fear, though, is futile and only feeds the stress, which triggers the neurochemical changes, which bring on my shadowy nightmares. I have come a long way since I learned what death meant from my kitten, Oscar. I am learning not to fight, but letting go of trying to control the ever-changing flow of life. I practice being grateful in each moment and embracing whatever happens next, even when it's as difficult as our current challenging circumstances.

***Jennifer D. Diamond's** first published short story appears in the* Mindful Writers Retreat Anthology, Over the River and Through the Woods. *When not hiking, SUP boarding, or kayaking, Diamond is polishing her first YA novel,* How We Spin, *third place winner in the Pennwriters 2019 Novel Beginnings contest. Follow Diamond on Facebook @Jennifer.D.Diamond.writer, Instagram @jennifer_d_diamond_writer or find her blog at jenniferddiamondwriter.wordpress.com.*

Until This. Until Now

by Janet Cincotta

Today was pretty much a perfect day for me. I woke up early this morning, ate a light breakfast, meditated longer than usual, and took my (almost) daily five-mile walk in the brilliant sunshine, under a cloudless sky, while listening to beautiful music. Summer delighted me with birdsong and treated me to vibrant shades of translucent green. No one else was out.

It would have been perfect except for one problem. The rest of the world is suffering. The majority of humankind is sick, worried they will get sick, or grieving the loss of a loved one who has been sick. People are scared. Angry. Broken.

It is June here in central Pennsylvania. The year is 2020. It will go down in history as the year that hosted a worldwide pandemic no one saw coming, and no one knows how to navigate. More than nine million people have already tested positive for infection with the novel SARS virus, Covid-19, that has already left almost 500,000 of them dead. There is no known cure for Covid-19, and no vaccine against it, so we are left to observe rituals we can only hope will contain its spread. We have been told to stay in our homes except to get food and medicine. We're required to wear face masks whenever we go out, keep our distance from other human beings, and wash our hands long, hard, and often.

The Covid-19 pandemic has touched us in ways we couldn't have imagined just a few months ago. From disbelief to fear, from exhaustion to illness, from confusion to grief to anger to despair, it has invaded every aspect of our lives. We weren't prepared for schools and businesses to close. We never thought we'd have to worry about running out of food and supplies. We believed our health care system was infallible. We thought we were pretty safe.

Until this. Until now.

Back in March, I celebrated the Ides by closing my door to the rest of the world. I'd forgotten that this was the day Shakespeare dispatched the soothsayer to warn Julius Caesar his life was in danger, and he should stay at home. Still, I sensed a great looming danger on the horizon. It sounded like good advice.

I surrendered my seat for the symphony that night just to be on the safe side. I figured out how to order groceries online and have them delivered to my front porch, so I didn't have to venture out for food. I canceled a dinner date with a friend, and I arranged to ship the presents I'd wrapped for my grandson because I knew I was going to miss his birthday party as he turned five. I withdrew my registration for a writing conference that I have attended every summer for the past four years—all the things I had planned and looked forward to with eager anticipation.

Until this. Until now.

Nevertheless, not much else has changed for me over the past few months, not the way it has for so many others. For people who have lost their jobs or closed their businesses. For parents who are still trying to hold down full-time jobs from home while they school their children, feed their families three meals a day plus snacks, and keep the house habitable. For essential workers who get up every day and march out into the germ-infested world to make things easier and safer for the rest of us, preparing and trucking the food and supplies we depend upon, and packing and delivering the orders we place from the comfort and shelter of our own homes. Manning the food banks, and treating the sick and dying in our hospitals and nursing homes. Worrying they will pick up the virus and carry it home to their children.

I don't have to worry about that, though. My children are grown and out on their own. I retired a couple of years ago, and I live alone now, so I'm accustomed to social distancing. I appreciate solitude, so isolation doesn't worry me. I've managed to tackle a few jobs around the house that needed attention. I'm reading through a stack of books that have been collecting dust in the back of my closet for years. I'm learning to meditate, trying to write. Doing what introverts and loners do best, living quietly and peacefully. Enjoying solitude, embracing uncertainty, and holding onto hope.

Which, I have always believed, is how healing begins by holding onto hope.

Until this. Until now.

Hope has taken on a new meaning for me. I had hoped to join the army of brave, dedicated doctors and nurses who are out there on the front lines in the battle against this unseen enemy. I had hoped to do my part because I'm a physician, meaning I am fully qualified and capable of pitching in to support them except for one problem. I'm also an official card-carrying member of the Covid-19 high-risk population, meaning my body can't churn out the kind of antibodies I would need to fight the infection if I picked it up somewhere. I would be doomed, so I've been asked to step away just because I'm old. Despite a compelling sense of duty, of urgency, of longing, I have been banished from joining my colleagues who are hard at work saving lives in the hospital where I practiced medicine for over thirty years. Meaning, I can't help at all.

Which, I believe, is what we were put here to do. To help.

Until this. Until now.

Since that day in March, when I closed my door to the world, my daughter and my grandson celebrated birthdays, without me. My daughter gave birth to her second child without me. My best friend kept vigil at her husband's bedside as he was dying without me. I would have been there to help through all of it. I would have held their hands and prayed. I would have come bearing gifts and offering comfort.

Until this. Until now.

If I could do it, if it were safe, I would pack my bags today, open my door to the world again, and venture out. But I wouldn't run to the mall, or chance a workout at the gym. I wouldn't meet my friends for lunch at our neighborhood café or stray into the local bookstore. I would drive directly from my front door to my daughter's, where I know my grandson would be waiting for me. He would propel himself across the porch and down the steps, and fling himself into my open arms, calling out, "Oma, play with me!" And happily, I would.

Until this. Until now.

Janet Cincotta is an author and physician with over thirty years of experience in Family Medicine. She now occupies an empty nest, and writes for the pure joy of it.

Covid Schmovid – Let's Fish

by Rick Robinson

The possibility of being the recipient of a sneeze-induced, microscopic-sized, virus-laced particulate (that, by the way, ironically looks like Wilson from the movie *Cast Away*) has changed people's lives the globe. The entire world seems to be either searching for protective masks or railing against a government conspiracy that masks will lead to the downfall of Western Civilization as we know it. As for social distancing, its either bubble-boy or frat-like keggers on the beach. As with politics these days, there is no middle ground.

One large group of people seeing no change in their daily outdoor routine are those of us who are fishers. Those who practice the sport of fishing practically invented today's guidelines. We have been practicing COVID procedures since Jesus stood on the shore of the Sea of Tiberias and instructed Simon Peter to have his guys spread out and cast nets to the right side of his boat. Note, a good guide knows where to find fish.

Throughout the COVID pandemic, part of my near-daily routine is to spend an hour or so pestering fish. I have two small ponds within walking distance of my home and two lakes stocked with trout a short drive away. During the COVID crisis, I have regularly visited these spots without any fear of infection. It's because fishers have been social distancing, masking, and washing our hands forever.

First, and foremost, fishing is a sport specifically designed for social distancing. People purposefully spread out along the shore keep their lines from getting tangled up. And at every pond, river, or creek, each has their favorite space where they fish and protect that golden "honey hole" like Pooh Bear protects … well … honey. Once you get to "your spot," you spread out your chair and gear to protect a zone at least six feet wide.

To add to my own personal social distance protection, I fly fish. The whipping back and forth of a small barbed hook at the end of a fly line would cause most DC Comic superheroes to keep their distance.

Finally, just to ensure approaching virus spreaders keep their distance, I smoke cigars while I fish. Mark Twain once said something to the effect that he smoked cigars to keep mosquitos and most people at a distance. I think we smoke the same brand.

So, for the most part, no one gets near smoky me wildly slinging a San Juan worm over and over again into my favorite fishing hole.

And fishers have been wearing masks long before people started eating undercooked bats in China. In order to charge us a premium, fish apparel companies call these masks "buffs." Structurally, buffs are ultraviolet ray blocking 1980s tube-tops for your nostrils. All the fishers buy buffs to keep the sun off their face neck and ears. Along with UV protection, they come with the added benefit of keeping particulate from someone sneezing either in or out, depending on your perspective.

The masks and distance do not make us anti-social. We just have no idea what the other is saying.

GUY DOWN SHORE FOM ME: "I caught a bass on a blue lure."

ME: "No, I never smoked grass watching Ben Hur."

We both give each other a thumbs up so as not to be embarrassed.

Finally, have you ever smelled the hands of someone that has caught a fish on a hot summer day? We wash our hands – A LOT. I went trout fishing on the Cumberland River over the 4th of July. My nephew cut up the day's catch. Three days later, he was still trying to wash the smell off his hands. He is a teacher and I suspect when his school resumes classes, some kid will ask, "What's that smell?" Of course, he will have a mask on, so no one will have any earthly idea what he asked.

So as COVID continues its pandemic path, join me at the lake – just don't get near my spot.

With over four decades in law and national politics, **Rick Robinson's** *novels are as current as today's headlines. Robinson's manner of relating political life and the campaign trail to readers has earned him Amazon top seller status, often placing multiple books in the top 100 at the same time. Robinson's numerous writing accolades include being named International Independent Author of the year. Rick Robinson is a Zoom Into Books Author.*

Not What We Expected

by F.T. Pandora

I.

His widow stood in the front pew of St. Colette's next to my brother's casket. She bent down and kissed the blond head of her fidgeting granddaughter, who was pulling at her sleeve. She knew Katie, at two, would never remember her grandfather. The priest began the funeral. We all made the sign of the cross with Fr. Casnell.

Casnell is a slight, balding man of Eastern European stock who came late in life to be a priest. He is soft-spoken, with twinkling eyes, and is genuinely kind to everyone. He should have retired some years ago, but he loves the people and they love him. So he stays. Cathy and I had arrived early for the service and saw an older man with his back to us, vacuuming the carpeting at the rear of the church. The older man was Fr. Casnell. He did his best in light of the rules.

Everyone wore a mask. Every other pew was closed to ensure distancing. Sections were roped off. Instead of mourners being together to comfort each other and share how my brother influenced their lives, they were scattered around the church in a semicircle. Some were half a football field away. His fraternity brother, John, two hundred miles from home, rehearsed the reading he was assigned. When it was his turn, his mouth opened, but no words came. Again he tried to read the prayer and again, he failed; finally, he limped through the short passage. Only his wife could comfort him. A very difficult day for family and friends during the pandemic.

But my brother was not infected. He did not die from the virus. Still, the virus took its toll on him, on his wife, his children, his grandchild, and my family without infecting a single one of us. We laid him to rest on July 13. We had not anticipated the cruelty of the virus.

II.

In December of 2019, well before anyone we knew was concerned about a virulent pathogen that had escaped from a Wuhan research facility on the other side of the earth. I noticed that my much younger wife was having trouble keeping up with me hiking. As a trim, athletic woman, this was a surprising departure from the workout, biking, and hiking we enjoyed. She finally confessed to severe pain in her foot.

Mike, our primary care physician, pronounced her foot pain beyond his family practice limits and sent her to a surgeon. The surgeon was, as they say, tall, dark, and handsome. To remind people that he was a surgeon and never far from the operating room, he wore green scrubs, green surgical cap, green surgical mask draped around his neck and orange high top basketball shoes. It was no surprise to us that a surgeon recommended surgery. He said she needed an Arthrodesis. Big word for a bone fusion in her right foot. She needed the procedure to join the bones where arthritis had eaten away all the cartilage. We pretended to see it on the x-rays he showed. What we knew for sure was, when she walked, the bone on bone movement was terribly painful. The procedure would involve a small incision and the insertion of two ordinary-looking hardware store screws arranged in an "X" and drilled into the two bones. Tall, Dark and Handsome could not fit her into his surgery schedule until the early part of the New Year. Prior to the surgery date, she would "just have to live on pain pills, slippers, and limping around." Eventually, she received a surgery date in March. The recovery time, he explained, will be longer than you would expect, and for the first few weeks, he said, her leg would be raised even in bed. Of course, she would be confined to her home and unable to walk, shower, drive, travel, shop, or do anything else that might bring her joy, some restrictions would fall away in a few weeks and some might remain for twelve.

To help take her mind off the pain, we visited Cancun with our two granddaughters, our son, and daughter in law. In Cancun, we met two women in their 20s from Ukraine. They were traveling with a 60-year-old man they met through a newspaper ad he placed in Chicago, offering a free vacation for traveling companions to Mexico. They were in touch daily with friends in Europe. They were the first to mention the new virus to us, other than a lone CNN reporter on TV in the airport prior to our departure for Mexico. She casually mentioned the "China-virus." The twenty-somethings said their friends reported that the virus was wreaking havoc on the city of Wuhan. "Don't worry," the CNN reporter had said, "it's not as bad as SARS and it's only in one city."

At home, we discussed the fact that, according to Dr. TD&H, my wife could be immobile from the surgery for months. That would mean we needed to lay in food and essential supplies. COSTCO and Sam's Club are excellent places to buy large amounts of food staples and cleaning supplies. Prior to her surgery, we bought several shopping carts of everything we could think we'd need for a lengthy recovery.

The surgery was successful! The cast-wrap on her leg extended from her toes to her knee. Her mobility was reduced to almost zero. We arranged the sunroom as a convalescent center and TV room so she could get out of the bedroom.

The TV was now a constant companion. The reports of the increases in infections, the number of countries involved, and the number of deaths worldwide started to be a never-ending topic on every news channel. News of quarantines began to come from all corners of the world. Then the virus, running unchecked in multiple countries, began to dominate the news cycles. Experts were predicting this could spread to many more countries. News readers predicted hospitals would be overwhelmed soon and ventilators and supplies of personal protection equipment would run out.

How lucky are we? we thought. Without thinking about the virus, we stocked up on everything we thought we might need. We had a lot of cleaning supplies, detergent, hand soap, toilet tissue, and freezers stocked with food for the months we expected to be in our own "post-surgery quarantine." Zoom and Facetime were poor substitutes for being with our grandkids, but we knew we could manage that. We toasted our good fortune and went to bed the night after the surgery feeling as though we had now, perhaps unwittingly, "outsmarted" the virus, and that it would not affect our lives any more than the recovery from surgery we had been anticipating.

A few weeks later, my brother texted he was being admitted to the hospital. He had been successful in battling cancer for five years. We traveled with him the previous two years and he was upbeat and happy. Now he was losing weight and couldn't eat. He needed nutritional support. This is when the virus began to take charge.

Normally, we would have been with him to lend at least emotional support. But in this dangerous time, there had to be rules to protect staff and patients. Covid rules prohibited most visitors, even family. Worse, the rules throughout the hospital were sometimes not uniformly enforced. Sometimes they changed from day to day. Sympathy for families' concerns seemed to come in second in the face of the rules. Even the palliative unit became a less compassionate place.

Sometimes, even the spouse was shut out. Occasionally, young staff wanted to check about visitations with a supervisor who was off on the weekend. It seemed clear the staff was frustrated by constantly changing rules. At the end, if not for a brave nurse who called to a central checkpoint for permission, his wife may have had a "Sophie's Choice" in determining which of his two sons was permitted to say goodbye. Thank God, a nurse took a chance.

In the end, he died without his brother or his sister at his side. We were shut out of his death by rules required by the virus we thought we had "outsmarted." My brother's last hospitalization had been almost in isolation. He battled both his disease and the loneliness of the rules. Without infecting our family, without any issues of shortages of PPE, medications, ventilators, or ICU capacity and with weeks of planning to be locked down for months, Covid-19 still managed to defeat us in a most personal and painful way. Even the wake and funeral had to conform to the Covid rules, so the grieving was less personal and less bearable. It felt like the virus won.

All my life, my family celebrated on July 13 because it was Mom's birthday. Now, July 13 is a reminder of how the pandemic helped to break our hearts. This was definitely not what we expected.

Award winning author, **F. T. Pandora**, *was the Chief Legal Officer of the multihospital healthcare system, OhioHealth, for over 25 years. He was named multiple times by Cincinnati Magazine as a top 100 Lawyer in Ohio and received the Business First Lifetime Achievement Award as an attorney in 2011. He and his wife, Catherine, currently divide their time between their granddaughters, Ellie and Livia, and traveling in Europe. His first book, middle grade mystery* Revenge, *won Honorable Mention at the Florida Book Festival.*

Covid-19 Memoir

by Dick Vieth

The novel coronavirus emerged in Wuhan in December and rampaged through that Chinese city, leaving death and despair in its wake. The gruesomeness and deadliness of the disease sent shivers down my spine.

Still, Wuhan, I rationalized, is half a world away; Chinese epidemiologists claim to have contained it; and Chinese travelers can't enter the U.S.

With the threat thus neatly tucked away in a dark corner of my brain, I entered 2020 resolved to begin the New Year by expanding my circle of friends and participating in more of the myriad activities available in Willow Valley Communities (WVC). I registered for Tai Chi, for the Willow Valley concert series, and for "Writing from the Heart," which proved so inspiring that we persuaded the teacher to extend it a month.

I joined a nearby church attended by many WVC residents. Its Adult Bible Class challenged my thinking, and its after-church lunch group widened my circle of friends. During January and February I met twice as many new people as the previous decade in Willow Valley.

At the same time I continued meeting with my "Gang of Four," a weekly study/discussion group. We were an unlikely mix: Jim W., a pastor; Roger, an advertising consultant; Jim H., a counselor; and myself, a theologian. We had grown close, able to share anything.

I awoke every morning eager to tackle my whirlwind of activities.

Then suddenly covid-19 erased every one of these joys. The virus spread silently westward from Wuhan, girdling the globe to Europe in two short months and then leaping the Atlantic. Terrifying stories emerged from New York City.

America was totally unprepared. Insufficient beds, ventilators, masks, gowns, gloves, and swabs. With Washington's ineptitude, every state, county, and city was on its own.

Soon covid-19 struck Lancaster. Two-thirds of the county's fatalities came from nursing homes or retirement communities like WVC. Suddenly I had become a prime target!

Like most Americans, I didn't like using the word "evil," but how could you call a pandemic infecting 13 million people worldwide and killing half a million anything less than "evil"? Did others feel the same way?

I called my next-door neighbor.

"Do you use the word 'evil'?" I asked.

"Only when talking about you," she replied.

Ignoring the dig, I continued, "Is novel coronavirus evil?"

"Absolutely!"

"What about systemic racism?" Demonstrations protesting George Floyd's murder were raging in the streets. "Is racism evil?"

"Definitely!"

When WVC residents were advised to pair off and check on each other daily, she agreed to be my partner. We would telephone each other every morning.

"What will you do if I don't answer?" I asked.

"Call Security and tell them to bring a body bag," she quipped.

In late March WVC issued an edict isolating the community. No visitors from outside, and any resident who traveled outside the County had to self-quarantine for two weeks. That canceled our family Easter celebration in Baltimore.

Further restrictions followed: stay in place, no visiting, frequent hand-washing, safe distancing, masks in public spaces.

What a downer! We felt like prisoners locked in our cells.

Our immediate problems now became loneliness and boredom. Cabin fever began to set in.

Soon WVC launched its answer to boredom: a series of TV lectures, concerts, and special programs. I especially enjoyed lectures on DaVinci, Degas, and Cezanne; the canals of Venice and the Panama Canal; the Pharaohs, the Medici, and the Tsars. It was impossible to take in all the good programs!

Another antidote to loneliness was Zoom. With Zoom our Gang of Four could meet virtually. Conversation once again bounced back and forth among us. We dissected readings and wrestled with current events, but our priority was sharing each other's joys and sorrows.

During one session, Jim H. noted that in covid-19 wards, people either die alone or die holding the hand of a stranger—a masked caretaker comforting them as they slip away.

"Would you rather die alone," I asked Roger, "or with your family present?"

"I'd want my wife there holding my hand." Roger answered.

"But if you go first, then she'll have to die alone."

"True. If I'm there for her when she goes, maybe I'd have courage to face dying alone."

Zoom also brought back "Writing from the Heart." Laughter and occasionally tears filled the screen as we recovered meaningful memories.

And Zoom allowed my clan to gather virtually. My two oldest grandsons displayed the product of their labors in quarantine: painting the house interior with their father. My other two grandkids showed off, Ovie, their Labrador retriever rescued from a Lab shelter. Ovie bounced around the screen, licking faces.

Even before all this took place, creative juices began flowing in my cul-de-sac, which consists of eleven houses surrounding a circular road. "Let's gather every Saturday at 5:00," one of our residents suggested. "Put on your mask, set your chairs six feet apart in a circle, and we'll have a party!"

The first Saturday was so much fun we stayed until descending darkness drove us back into our isolation booths. The following Saturday a resident from the next cul-de-sac sneaked in. "I heard your laughter last week and had to crash the party!"

In June we planned a surprise for a resident with a special connection to a Roman summer solstice festival. Ideas sparked from person to person as the festival took shape. An eternal flame was central to the ancient festival, so I asked permission to have a small charcoal fire.

"Absolutely not!" the administrator declared.

"Well, then, how about Tiki torches?"

"Hmmm. I'm not saying yes, but I'm not saying no."

Permission granted!

Everything came off beautifully. The astonished roastee said she hadn't had so much fun in months.

Independence Day fell on Saturday a few weeks later. I suggested we plan our own Fourth of July. Response was lukewarm.

"Who'll volunteer to take charge?" I asked.

"It's your idea, so you do it," came the unanimous response.

I did have an idea. Covid-19 had exposed America's institutional racism, and George Floyd's murder rubbed it raw. White America was waking up to four centuries of Black oppression. "This year's celebration," I proposed, "should highlight the dark underside of American history."

We opened with a recording of "Stars and Stripes Forever" and readings from the Declaration of Independence and the Gettysburg Address. A resident then read Caroline Randall Williams stunning op-ed from the *New York Times*, "My Body is a Confederate Monument," and another read Abel Meeropol's bombshell poem, "Strange Fruit." I followed with Martin Luther King's "I Have a Dream," and we sang the Black National Anthem, "Lift Every Voice and Sing." The program concluded with fireworks displayed on a laptop. People stayed another hour, enjoying each other's company. We were beginning to bond. As we broke up, one participant said, "I'm going to miss these gatherings when they come to an end."

The next morning we were surprised to find a feature essay on "Lift Every Voice" prominently displayed on the front page of the Sunday Lancaster paper. I immediately emailed my thanks to the author, Jeff Hawkes, attaching a copy of our program. He replied, "I think your Independence Day program was spot on—stirring, meaningful and thought-provoking."

During one of our family Zoom meetings, my son remarked, "Because of the lockdown our family has done more things together, and we've grown closer." I, too, have found such unanticipated side-effects. Indeed, my experience of our six-month lockdown has been as much positive as negative, largely, I suppose, because the virus hasn't touched me personally.

That is, until a recent Zoom meeting of the Gang of Four. Three of us appeared on screen, but not Roger. A phone call revealed that he was in the ICU with severe anemia. Tests disclosed he also had something more scary: a positive reading for the novel coronavirus. That took the air out of my lungs. Suddenly the virus was blowing its hot breath in *our* faces.

"Did you have any symptoms?" I asked Roger.

"No. It was a complete surprise."

"What caused it?"

"I haven't a clue. We've been so cautious we haven't even gone shopping. Groceries and meds are delivered outside our door."

How capricious this pandemic is, I thought, sneaking in where we least expect it.

The following week Roger appeared on screen looking strong as ever. "Still no symptoms," he said. We breathed a collective sigh of relief, but saved celebration until his fourteen-day quarantine concludes.

Even then any celebration will be muted by the upturn in new cases in our county, state, and nation. Dr. Fauci says the spike is not the "second wave," just the end of the beginning of the first wave. We've got a long way to go.

Richard F. Vieth *has served as a parish pastor, campus pastor, and, most recently, professor of theology at Lancaster Theological Seminary. He was married to his wife Jean for 61 years until her recent death. He has two sons and four grandchildren. Now retired in Willow Valley Communities, he is working on his memoir, centered on his participation in the Selma march for voting rights.*

A Memoir in a Time of Upheaval

by Connie Cousins

The last three months have felt like a whirlwind with no calming in sight. My heart ached with sympathy for the pandemic victims and filled with pride because of the dedication of front-line workers.

I watched first with interest and then with horror as COVID-19 took over the news. Then came the quarantine orders and the strangeness of not hopping in the car and going to Walmart or having dinner out. The days blended into an extensive line of sameness while the numbers of infected rose and I waited for my copy of a reenacted nursing license.

Wearing a mask didn't bother me as it did other people because, for nearly 40 years, I worked as a CRNA (Certified Registered Nurse Anesthetist) and worc PPE of some type every day, but always the mask.

I found that much good was coming out in acts of kindness among people worldwide. Entire families were home at the same time—working, studying, attending class–all of it challenging. But, in the slowdown, people also listened to each other and got reacquainted.

For me, it has been a time of gradual slowing and prioritizing like I've never done before. I gave myself permission to be still, meditate, and read. At a different pace, I also wrote and put the final changes on a children's book I have worked on, off and on, for years.

As people began to adjust to the shut-down methods, they suddenly faced a new scene of brutality. The killing of George Floyd at the hand of a policeman, or rather his knee to Floyd's neck, produced shock and outrage. Protesters filled streets in cities in the United States and globally.

My reaction was based on my own experiences growing up–like most people today.

As I grew up, I never had a single black person in my classes. A neighboring town was home to a few Blacks—mostly from the same family. The community treated them fairly as far as I knew.

I reported for my first summer job in 1956. I worked at a drive-in ice cream stand from age 14 through my high school years. On one of my first days on the job, my boss said, "If those Negroes come in here, you give them a paper cup–not one of our frosted root beer mugs! I asked why, but she just repeated her orders and said, "That's the way it is."

I could not accept this. I had not been around Blacks, but my gut told me this was wrong! She was stingy as well and insisted we weigh each ice cream cone.

When the boss lady wasn't there, I gave each person who ordered root beer a frosted mug.

I did not feel for years that I had any prejudice, but was I ever tested? Not really.

As a young nurse, I only remember curiosity about my patients regardless of their skin color. I examined their hair products and admired the beautiful skin of the young women.

When riots erupted in the 1960s, I had many mixed feelings. My husband, a state policeman, worked during the uprisings in Pittsburgh. I worried about him and wondered if things were as bad for the Blacks as they claimed. I didn't understand why there couldn't have been more gradual integration etc. to prevent discord.

In the 70s. I saw troopers admitted to police academies with lower scores and the same type of things in my nurse anesthesia school. One day a black student, an underclassman, told two other anesthetists and me, "I'm not too worried. The NAACP will back me." He was talking about failing a recent exam. Unfortunately, his next trick was sniffing the gas from a gas machine in a vacant operating room early one morning. Dismissal came swiftly.

From that experience, I developed a simmering level of distrust and suspicion when dealing with Blacks. I never felt that Blacks were inferior, but after those years and the resulting efforts to desegregate schools and the working world, something changed. In my husband's world, I saw black police officers promoted over white guys and women with more years and higher test scores. I secretly felt the government and the states were giving Blacks a leg up–whether they deserved it or not. How would this help the underlying problems?

I'm not saying anything is, or was fair, regarding health care. It has always been obvious that poverty is difficult to overcome, and health care suffers as a result. I have always supported head-start programs and things like that as well as non-profits, both local and national.

My own four children also attended schools with few Blacks. Race relations were just not on our radar. My one son counted a black girl among his friends in college. She occasionally came to the house for a weekend with other young people. She was lovely and I hope we didn't cause her to feel out of place.

So fast forward this woman to age 77 and I have had to take another look at my view, my beliefs, and my actions. I've always been horrified to see unfair treatment by law enforcement, but it was–out there somewhere–not something I had to do anything about. The worst thing I heard about when my husband was a cop was a story about one of the police who had used his flashlight on the head of a young man, known to all the force as a troublemaker. People repeated that story because the young man himself told it and said, "That cop really got my attention. I straightened up after that." I don't think I stopped to think, *Hey, that was wrong–he could have caused brain damage.*

So now I wonder, "How did we get to this point where a wrestle to the ground or a threat turns into murder?" Has the world turned a blind eye for so long that nothing phases it? So, I ask myself, "What could I possibly do to help the situation?

During this wild ride of pandemic plus brutality on the streets, I will, to the best of my ability to listen, write to congressmen and women–in other words–DO Something.

I think the time I have spent recently with tears in my eyes may have been a start, but I have a long way to go to understand or walk in a black woman's shoes.

My first order of business to be a better neighbor was to question my only black friend about the various groups supporting the protests. I wanted to know if Black Lives Matter was doing good works, in her opinion. She gave me several websites to check out. This weekend, the protests to commemorate a young man's death last year by a police officer were orderly and meaningful. I plan to go to the next one which high school students planned later this week.

No, I *can't* understand, but I *can* stand and *take a stand* behind and *with* the Black citizens of our community.

Just like the pandemic we're still in the middle of, education is the key. So many people didn't understand why wearing a mask was important. I heard many times, "I seldom go out and I'm okay. If I get sick, it'll be my fault." That is true, but it is also very selfish. Those people, not believing in the science, or feeling it's their choice only, are putting those of us who live near or work with them in danger every day.

Thank goodness, most people have gone the way of serving their fellow man and their neighbors during COVID. They pick up groceries, they give generously to food banks, they check on neighbors, they offer to pick up someone having work done on a car, or anything else they can do to help.

These good neighbors are also on the front lines and serving in their own way.

We will get through this with faith, energy, and ingenuity!

***Connie Cousins** is a retired CRNA(Certified Registered Nurse Anesthetist) and renewed her RN license when COVID-19 moved into the area. She is a mother of four and grandmother of nine wonderful people. She has written for the* Centre County Gazette *for several years. Her blog is clcousins.com.*

We Go Through It

by Lisa McCombs

Diagnosed with multiple sclerosis in 2001, my life has become increasingly reclusive over the years; so when COVID 19 decided to visit the USA, things didn't change drastically for me. Or, so I thought. All of a sudden, I missed a social life I hadn't realized existed.

My COVID19 journey began in late February 2020. My parents and I planned to visit Dad's sister in the state capital, where she resided. Whenever I have a book event there, we always take advantage of the opportunity to spend time with her. Retired and alone, she usually welcomed us with open arms. I always enjoyed these visits. A self-proclaimed career gal, Aunt Sandra lived a rather lavish life of southern values. She had a SITTING room. Where people came to SIT!

The beauty of her home always soothed me and inspired me to perfect my own home's aesthetics.

The day before our departure on the two-hour drive south, my aunt's friend called to let us know that Aunt Sandra was in the hospital with pneumonia.

We stopped at the hospital en route to Sandra's house to find a shriveled version of my six foot one, 83-year-old aunt. Having suffered from rheumatoid arthritis all her life, she had always managed to camouflage the twisted body parts now prominent in the silhouette tangled in the sheets of the hospital bed.

She was alert, though. She knew us and was fast to apologize for not greeting us with a cake, as all good Methodist women prepared for guests. This lapse in proper social etiquette seemed to disturb her more than her medical situation.

She didn't particularly look well, but she also didn't appear to be on death's door. We left her two hours later in search of sustenance, promising to return the next day.

4:00 a.m., Friday, February 21, 2020, the phone woke my parents and me. Sandra Lee Myers had passed in her sleep.

Two weeks later, the first confirmed case of COVID19 was reported in Kanawha County, home of West Virginia's state capital. I know what you're thinking. I don't have an answer.

By mid-March, college and university spring breaks were lengthened, followed by a state mandate that all classes would finish the semester with virtual instruction. My son's much-anticipated freshman year at WVU was cut short.

Not long after the state-wide closing of all public schools, my husband lost his job, putting us in the unemployment system with thousands of fellow Mountaineers. School children either rejoiced at the unexpected reprieve from the classroom or suffered through days without the security of that safe environment.

Americans glued themselves to the growing news of a widespread contagion covering our country. Businesses felt the sting of declined economic support. Hospitals were inundated with patients they didn't know how to treat. The shortage of hand sanitizer, antibacterial cleaners, and toilet paper lead to consumer hoarding.

After the initial concern about my family's future, my survival instinct kicked in, and I got busy. Instead of wallowing in self-pity and negativity, I decided to take advantage of the government's request to stay home. I finished writing my next young adult novel. I worked diligently on my writing. I spent every morning with my diary, posted on my blog, or visited the lives of my fictional characters. Writing has always calmed me and there was no better time to seek solace.

When I wasn't writing, I knitted three baby blankets and learned that I will probably *never* successfully knit a sock. By

May 1, I had exhausted my Netflix addiction and moved on to the Prime network. When I finally tired of the wasted life, I decided to convert spare time into physical fitness. I began exercising daily, starting with AM stretches, midday Body Groove sessions, and evening physical therapy moves learned from previous sessions in the gym. Unfortunately, all of this self-love usually turned into a junk food feeding frenzy, 'cause I "deserved it."

Social media became my best friend. Facebook offered a community of like-minded folks: MS Warriors, book geeks, writer friends, fellow parents, free knitting patterns, FAMILY, church services…It was all there. When Facebook didn't suffice, I learned about Instagram (My nieces have already pointed out how technically behind I am.), Twitter, and Zoom events.

Amazon on-line shopping gave me the instant gratification through the United States Postal Service that this Pandemic warrior needed. Who *doesn't* like getting packages in the mail? For three+ months I enjoyed weekly deliveries right to my front door. At first, my credit card bill was a concern; then, I discovered the advantages of having Amazon Prime. I am now an Amazon junky. With my Prime membership, I get free music downloads, access to movies, and purchase BONUSES that really add up.

The Pandemic (my very first and hopefully my last) also turned me into a 21st century Gladys Kravitz, the iconic neighborhood snoop on the old "Bewitched" sit-com. I spent hours a day in my rocking chair gazing out at my lovely little neighborhood. I had a first-row seat for rainstorms, suspicious foot travel, mail deliveries, and the Great 2020 Hydrangea Theft on McCue Avenue. My elderly neighbors across the street effortlessly cultivate seasonal flora. I love looking out at the assortment of color from my non-green thumb existence.

One early evening, I happened to glance outside the living room window to witness a young girl-child pull over on her bicycle, fling it to the ground, rush up to Ruth's front garden and snatch a dark purple hydrangea before riding away with a glance over her shoulder. At first, I smiled at the prank. Then she came back and grabbed two more blooms without even looking around for witnesses. The audacity! Once was cute. Twice was criminal.

At this point, I am befuddled. What do I do? Open the front door and confront her? Report the crime to the neighbors? Alert the town cop of the incident? Not certain of flower-theft protocol, I did nothing; but I did keep a vigilant eye on further activity across the street.

If I felt helpless prior to Corona 2020, the self-preservation lesson I received during this event reinforced in me an uncomfortable dependence. Already aware of my MS reality, the equation of COVID 19 + Multiple Sclerosis left me paranoid, afraid, and anxious. For weeks I clipped disease- monitoring newspaper articles for my daily journal.

Then the local newspaper stopped going to print every day, revealing another scary truth. A shortage of cleaning supplies, toilet paper, bottled water, and paper towels ravaged the area while grocery aisles became empty. Small business owners went bankrupt while alcohol consumption grew. I wasn't totally convinced that this wasn't the Biblically promised Apocalypse.

By July, the fate of schools resuming in the fall was unresolved. Sporting events across the nation were canceled. Positive cases of Covid 19 spiked once again. The world, as we once knew it had become a masked society.

What were we to do? In the words of children's author Michael Rosen, "We can't go over it. We can't go under it. Oh no! We've got to go through it!" (*We're Going on a Bear Hunt*, 1989). That's what we Americans do. We work through it. It looked like I had more time to work on that knitted sock.

Lisa A. McCombs *has fulfilled her life with a successful 33 year teaching career. She is a Readers Favorite award-winning author of young adult fiction with books that include* Abby, Raspberry Beret, Opening Pandora's Box, Bombs Bursting in Air, *and* Praise Petals. *Lisa was diagnosed with multiple sclerosis in 2001 and is the author of the multiple award-winning book,* I Have MS: What's Your Super Power? *is her nonfiction debut. Lisa McCombs is a Zoom Into Books Author.*

Nature Is Always Open

by Suzanne Alexander

On New Year's Day 2020, there were rumblings of a pandemic on the loose. It didn't take long for this new virus to spread to people around the world. By the middle of March, residents in most of the United States were under orders to lock down to prevent this novel coronavirus from spreading. However, Mother Nature never received this directive to "stay at home." Nature was ready to come out of her winter sleep, no matter what.

In spite of the disease's specter shadowing our state and country, my husband and I were feeling the blessings of being surrounded by nature. Serene woods were our neighbors, and they were ready to put on a spectacular show to replace the closed theaters and other entertainment venues.

Sunny yellow daffodils popped out of the ground in March to give us something to smile about. I cut a bouquet to cheer up the inside of our home. Even Spice Cat seemed pleased. She had been eyeing us with suspicion. "What are you doing around here so much?" her meows seemed to convey.

With their vibrant pink flowers, redbud trees showed off their blossoms at the edge of the woods. Later, they unfurled their heart-shaped leaves—nature's gift of love.

At that same time, bluebirds were checking out the blue birdhouse, specially designed for them. In and out they flew, carrying dried grass and twigs to turn their house into a comfy home.

"Bluebird carries the sky on his back," essayist, poet, and philosopher Henry David Thoreau once said. And their blue sky backs were needed as April brought cold and clouds, a depressing pallor matching the world news.

At that time, we switched from winter's oily black sunflower seed in our bird feeder to dried mealworms, thanks to Walmart being open. The bluebirds seemed happy with the new menu, taking breaks throughout the day from their nest building activity to fortify themselves.

Since a museum is not an essential business as is Walmart, the Huntington Museum of Art, over the Ohio River in Huntington, West Virginia, was closed – but not the nature trails surrounding it. Needing a change of scenery and to give Spice Cat a respite from her humans, Ron and I bundled up in the unusual cold. We headed up a hill in Huntington to the museum to check out nature's show around it.

With camera in tow, I captured what looked like pink splashed petals on a dogwood tree at the trail's entrance. I discovered these petals are leaves called bracts that surround the tiny, greenish-white flowers in the middle. The flowers will produce red berries in the autumn, providing food for hungry birds.

Farther down on the nature trail, we came upon stark white and dark purple trillium in bloom. These wildflowers are nicknamed "wake robin" because they, like robins, herald spring in various areas of the country. With the colors, lines, and textures of the flowers and leaves, it was obvious that some art had escaped the closed museum to make its way along the trail. Following the golden rule, we left the trail, "taking only pictures, leaving only footprints."

A cold April turned into an equally freezing May Day. Clusters of white flowers on our Viburnum bush resembled snowballs, the bush's nickname, which matched the prediction of snow flurries. The forecast also coincided with the cold, depressing news of the virus. However, unlike the news, the weather warmed and nature was determined to show more of its cheery colors.

Ron discovered an Eastern Box Turtle, with its shell splashed with orange, on our lawn as he prepared to mow. Mowing was still a must, even in a pandemic. The turtle munched on a strawberry that I fed it and then sought refuge under our deck.

By Mother's Day, the female bluebird was having a hectic celebration. Both she and her partner were frantically taking turns hunting for insects for their hatchlings. We kept a supply of mealworms available in the feeder, and I did my best to try to catch photos of the busy birds.

Mother's Day morning made my attempts easier. Ron presented me with a Bird Photo Booth, a feeder, and motion-activated camera combination. What fun! Something else to focus on other than the looming virus. Before too long, I captured photos of Carolina wrens, with their white eye stripes, ruddy backs, and short, almost vertical tails, feeding on mealworms. Of course, our resident bluebirds, including the fledglings, were ready for their close-ups as well, including ones with them holding fat mealworms in their beaks.

While the fledglings were out of the nest and flying about our woods and yard, the empty birdhouse appeared to have signaled the first-ever sighting of tree swallows. In the fifteen years we have lived on this property, we had never seen a tree swallow with iridescent blue feathers on its back and snowy white feathers below. It was time to get the bird book off the shelves.

We learned that tree swallows nest in bluebird houses, too, and they had their eyes on this home. It was a battle of wills between the bluebirds and swallows as to who would occupy the house next. The tree swallows eventually won. That was until the hot summer weather arrived and the tree swallows disappeared.

Nevertheless, once the hummingbird feeder was up, we had new residents. My homemade nectar lured first a male Ruby-throated hummingbird, and a pale female followed him. Unlike the tree swallows, the pair have stayed and are a welcome presence.

The world outside our yard and woods have changed, but nature has stayed pretty consistent – except for one disturbing fact. The milkweed is blooming, but the monarch butterflies we see every year flitting around the flowers have not returned. As a matter-of-fact, there are no butterflies at all around our flourishing garden. They seem to be keeping a far "social distance." Maybe they will return next summer when, hopefully, the pandemic is under control and life is back to normal or close to it. Then we can all celebrate with the butterflies and Mother Nature.

Suzanne Alexander *is the author of award-winning Through Children's Eyes: Exploring the Huntington Museum of Art and newly released, The Tip of the Tale. She is a docent at the Huntington Museum of Art in Huntington, WV. Suzanne Alexander is a Zoom Into Books Author.*

Strength of Small Towns

by Don Stansberry

9/11. Like most Americans, I remember that day with shock and anger. The images of the planes, the fire, and the people covered in dust still linger. But, with all that, one of the things that sticks in my mind is what most newsmen were reporting: America would never be the same. They were wrong. Fortunately, my day to day life has not changed one bit. Okay, it may take a little longer to get on a plane now, but besides that, my existence has been the same.

I think this virus may be different

2020 started badly for me with the death of Kobi Bryant. I am not much of a news person, but I did watch TV as the terrible news of the helicopter crash worsened. Around that time, we became aware of something happening in China, but then it seemed like there was always something happening in that part of the world. It was not unusual to see people scurrying through cities wearing masks. I gave it little thought.

I am a sucker for a good conspiracy theory. My wife came across a story about a doctor in China who was angering government officials by telling anyone who would listen about a virus that was killing people in Wuhan. What made it more interesting was that this whistleblower ended up dying of the virus (or being killed by the Chinese government, which makes an even better story). Then the Chinese started dropping like flies, which was terrible, but have you seen some of those fish markets? I figured it was a wonder that even a virus could survive there.

Then the virus started showing up in Germany, France, and boom! It was like a Stephen King novel. We looked at photos of the empty streets and plazas and wild animals roaming the streets of India. We saw the people on their balconies singing or doing anything that might fight the illusion of isolation. Watching the TV, the world seemed to be going down the tubes: looking out my window, everything was great.

After Christmas, my daughter had gone back to college, along with all students coming back from China and Europe. That was a bit of a concern. If she did get the virus, would she be allowed to come home? Would we be allowed to go there? Who thought we would ever be worried about something like this?

By the end of February, I had stopped worrying about it. My wife was worrying enough for the both of us. I went back to Seinfeld, Monk, and the NBA as my nightly entertainment.

As the cases started showing up in the U.S., we forgot about Europe, China, and anyone else who might be suffering. We started watching the stats. Positive cases, the number of people tested, deaths. All the news outlets had them, even the Weather Channel. I think everyone found the platform that gave the worst numbers and decided it was the most correct.

I have been in the public school system for almost 40 years, and I feel (probably incorrectly) that I am immune to nearly everything. So, when we started hearing rumors our county was going to have a preemptive shut down for a week. I could hardly believe it. There had been times when the classrooms were less than half full because of the flu, and we had not shut down.

One week became two, and we needed to find a way to teach the students remotely. One of the problems was they went home on a Friday, not knowing school had been canceled. Their books were at school, so they were useless as a teaching tool. We had no way of knowing who had internet access at home. We created packets with lessons, asked parents to pick them up at designated times, and coordinated food giveaways with some of the packet pick up times. But we really could not grade any returned work for fear it could be contaminated. The lessons planned online were great, but eventually, most kids stopped doing them. Who could blame them? They knew the grades were going to stop after the third semester.

We continued the food handouts and had a forty-car parade of teachers and staff driving through our district blowing horns and waving to the families of our students who stood in their yards waving back. Causing havoc and noise in their neighborhoods was our way of showing we cared, I guess.

So, here we are now, kind of at an impasse. We have had the restrictions lessened then after a few weeks tightened. I do love the chaos. People want answers from the government when there are none. They want someone to take care of them. They want the government to DO SOMETHING. But not so much here in West Virginia.

I love West Virginia, I really do. I could not imagine living anywhere else. What is the first thing we rush out to buy when the Pandemic hits? Toilet paper and bullets. It makes sense to me. We are a practical kind of people. When the real epidemic hits, who is going to survive? We are.

I think the gap in this country is not so much between rich and poor, black, or white, but between the big city and the rest of us. The Pandemic has illuminated that fact for me. I still think the true strength of this country lies in the small towns and communities that make up the U.S. That's not what we see on the news. Try watching it in that light.

For me, this has been one of the best times of my life. Thirty years of marriage, I have never gotten to spend so much time with my wife. I have been able to work out nearly every day (even when the gyms were closed), I had a key. Got to love West Virginians and their respect for the rules. Maybe, most importantly, I have had time to think. COVID 19 has been my Walden Pond.

I have had phone conversations instead of texts and talked to neighborhood families as they have walked through the neighborhood. I have been able to write some short stories and finished up my part of a new children's book.

Initially, pollution worldwide went down. It was fun to see the before and after pictures. But now the landfills are overflowing with take-out containers and Amazon packaging. I am not really a computer person, but it would have been interesting to see how we would have fared without online ordering for food and merchandise. It became a pastime for many.

The worst part is the masks. I will not rant. I will just say most doctors I've talked to say if you are wearing a mask, you are not going to be any more protected if the person next to you is or isn't wearing one. If you think two masks are better that one, then wear two, one right over the other.

I remember a time a couple of years ago when people, even some seemingly intelligent people, were going on about a zombie apocalypse. I think it is here. I see mask wearers moving slowly with dead eyes through stores. It is hard to talk, so no one does. I have walked right by people whom I've known well without speaking because I wasn't sure it was them. Put on a hat with a mask and everyone looks alike. I guess those stagecoach robbers knew what they were doing.

I figure we are all going to get the virus sometime or other. The prevention now is not really a prevention, it is just a slowdown of the virus, so the hospitals will not be inundated with cases. Then it will come around again every year like the flu or the avian flu. Around 35,000 people died of the flu in 2018. I wonder if we can estimate COVID 19, taking that number each year. I know we might have a vaccination by next year, but we also have one for the flu right now.

Just as generals know they will lose men on dangerous missions, we will sacrifice a few to the virus to get the economy back up and running. I think that is why there is pressure to lessen the restrictions. After all, nearly 37,000 people die in automobile accidents in the U.S. each year and we have not banned cars.

Each generation loses something but gains something else. We may have lost the custom of shaking hands for good, smiling at each other in the grocery store, and hugging an old friend. Those things were important to us. They may be forgotten by the next generation. Our society will have lived through this Pandemic and changed with it, hopefully for the better.

Don Stansberry is an international award-winning author of the YA Inky Series, Secret Blood, Vulture Bend, Crusty*, and* Skipping Through the ABC's of History*. He is a retired elementary school teacher and basketball coach. Don Stansberry is a Zoom Into Books Author.*

What I Did During My Covid-19 Vacation

by Edwin Daryl Michael

My wife and I were on a memorable Viking Cruise to the Panama Canal in late February when news of the ominous COVID-19 virus began appearing on TV. The threat of being quarantined on a cruise ship was quite disturbing. We couldn't imagine being "isolated" in our small, 10' by 20' room, with all meals delivered to our door. The only consolation was that we could have spent hours on our private balcony watching for flying fish, or frigate birds, or porpoises, and scanning the heavens for constellations and shooting stars. My wife and I are very good friends, and enjoy each other's company. But, neither of us wanted such close contact for days or weeks. There was a limit to our tolerance.

Our cruise ended the first week of March, and with masks, hand sanitizers, wipes, and gloves, we flew safely into the Pittsburgh airport – a short time before many cruise ships were prevented from docking. I have a comprised immune system due to the presence of T-cell lymphoma. Upon returning to Morgantown, my personal physician warned me to avoid exposure to the Covid virus – or any type of virus. She advised, "Ed, you must avoid all crowds and even small groups of people. Under no circumstances should you go into a restaurant, grocery store, or hospital."

My wife and I typically enjoy a night out once a week, visiting a restaurant and filling our plates from the salad bar. That came to an end in March, as did my trips to basketball games, the post office, library, church, and my barber, dentist, and dermatologist. My wife became proficient at ordering groceries online and waiting patiently to pick them up curbside. And, of course, she greatly increased her online ordering of non-grocery items. Our garage was so crowded with cardboard boxes we had difficulty making our way to the storage shelves.

In spite of all the restrictions, I did not suffer during the months when we were advised to wear masks, avoid crowds, and wash our hands hourly. I was fortunate to have a computer in front of a large window in my finished basement and to have over a cord of dry ash firewood stacked just outside my basement door. I enjoyed the daily task of keeping my woodstove glowing, hauling ashes onto my garden, and refilling bird feeders. Winter residents such as blue jays, cardinals, chickadees, finches, and titmice kept me entertained for hours. Two suet feeders attached to readily visible trees attracted a variety of woodpeckers, ranging from the small downy to the mid-sized red-bellied, and to the largest of them all, the pileated. Chipmunks, gray squirrels, white-tailed deer, and wild turkeys were also frequent visitors.

Birds were not aware of the threats we humans faced from the virus, and their annual cycles continued as if the world was a safe place to live. Birds that had migrated to the south the previous autumn began returning to their summer homes in April, and my black oil sunflower seeds attracted dozens of rose-breasted grosbeaks, towhees, and nuthatches. I was also entertained by brown thrashers, gray catbirds, house wrens, and hummingbirds. My daily bird diary documented the arrival of countless warblers, thrushes, and vireos, which foraged the treetops in the wooded area behind my house. Bird watching/listening was one hobby still available to persons who lived within walking distance of a park or within easy driving distance of a larger natural area. Waterfowl were returning from their winter homes in the south and small lakes served as stopover rest areas for thousands of individuals. Bars, fitness centers, movie theaters, and restaurants might have been closed to crowds of humans, but nature never closed its doors. And, there was no reason for a person to wear a mask while wandering in search of birds.

A second major hobby that proved rewarding and carried few restrictions was gardening. In March, I sowed 50 tiny tomato seeds in small plastic containers, which were set in south-facing windows. Those required little care other than weekly watering. Included were seeds of the famous WV 63, a hybrid tomato bred and developed by Manon Gallegly, a West Virginia University professor. After 13 years of selective breeding, Dr. Gallegly introduced his blight-resistant variety in 1963, to celebrate the 100th anniversary of West Virginia becoming a state.

In addition to sowing tomato seeds, I spaded a small section of my garden and planted lettuce, spinach, and snap peas. Those vegetables tolerate days of cold and wet weather, plus frosts and light freezes. By April, the resulting rows of visible leaf lettuce, dark green spinach, and snap pea seedlings would have convinced most viewers that I was a real gardener. As the soil warmed and frosts became a rarity, I plowed the remainder of my small garden and planted bush beans, pole beans, and summer squash. By May, I transplanted nearly 30 small tomato seedlings into two garden rows, four large plastic pots, and deep black bark landscaping mulch at select, sunny sites around my house. One especially productive site was in front of my air conditioner. Yes, I know this sounds like a strange place to grow tomatoes, but it had been the most productive of all sites I utilized in previous years. For at least six years, I had a productive cherry tomato plant in front of my air conditioner. Last year, I harvested some 270 small, bright-red cherry tomatoes from that one plant. In each previous year, I had harvested at least 200 small juicy tomatoes. I have no explanation for this phenomenon, but it could possibly be due to the warm air that flows over the plant. I have 28 small green, marble-size tomatoes present now on my air conditioner plant, and expect to be picking ripe red ones by the end of July.

I picked several gallons of crisp leaf lettuce and spinach in April and May, but dry weather limited production. My snap peas were not a great success, although I did manage to harvest nearly three quarts. By the first of July, I had eight hills of healthy-looking acorn and butternut squash, with a couple of small marble-size baby squash visible. Pole beans were sending runners up the poles I had set in the ground, and a few of my tomato plants, including the one in front of the air conditioner, were over four feet tall. All had promising collections of blooms, which should result in a surplus of fresh tomatoes by the middle of August. Similar to previous years, I expect to begin depositing small baskets of ripe tomatoes on my neighbors' doorsteps by the first of September.

My bird watching/listening will continue all summer, as will my gardening efforts. Few hobbies can produce as much enjoyment and rewards as do these two. However, I was fortunate to have two additional hobbies that filled the hours when I might have otherwise been shopping or watching sports on TV – writing historical fiction and carving duck decoys. When it was too hot to work outside in the garden and when birds were resting quietly in the shade, I wrote or carved. I am finishing a novel entitled, "The Coyotes of Canaan," which describes the lives of a pack of coyotes that inhabit Canaan Valley and the Dolly Sods Plateau. I spent two years conducting research for this fictional novel and was able to complete the first rough draft in January. Four persons provided edits and reviews, and by July, I was almost ready to submit it to my wife, who had provided the invaluable edits for all previous novels.

My workshop contains three rough blanks of black walnut, awaiting my carving knives, chisels, drawknives, rasps, and wood burner. When completed, the resulting wooden decoys will closely resemble a Canada goose, a green-winged teal, and a mallard.

During my stay-at-home vacation, I also decluttered my workshop and basement office. Multiple trashcans of useless materials found their way curbside, awaiting the arrival of the weekly garbage truck. Thirty years of hoarding had produced dozens of boxes of near-useless items. Although convinced I would need many of the items in the coming days, weeks, months, or years, I forced myself to complete the task. I must admit it is somewhat comforting to walk into my workshop and see organized bins, boxes, pegboards, and shelves.

Despite the rather severe restrictions thrust upon me, the seven-month segment of my life (January-July, 2020) defined as the Covid-19 era was productive and rewarding. I may be one of the few individuals who lived during that period who did not feel their life had been torn asunder. I am fortunate to have remained healthy and to have rewarding hobbies to fill my days and nights. However, I will not regret the ending of this threat and hope I can take my wife out to dinner before the year ends.

Ed Michael *is the author of The Missing Hand, a YA novel and A Valley Called Canaan: 1885-2002 and The Last Appalachian Wolf. His 50-year career as a wildlife biologist resulted in more than 100 publications, both scientific and popular. One of his major contributions involved surveys to document the distribution, life history, and ecology of the endangered, West Virginia northern flying squirrel. Dr. Michael continues to be an active outdoorsman, researcher, and writer, concentrating his efforts on wildlife of the central Appalachian Mountains.*

Hello, Your Anxiety Is Calling

by Donna Leiss

My husband's work cell phone rang and I knew it was one of those life-changing calls. Anxiety tore through my chest and belly. I knew the feeling well; I was born in fear. When my mom was in the throes of childbirth with me, the doctor found no pulse and pronounced me dead. My mom ignored him and thrust me into the world. The room was deathly silent until the doctor smacked my bottom, prompting my cry of life. It unnerved me being declared dead before I'd even made an entrance.

"That was work," Todd said in an unusually quiet tone, confirming my gut reaction. "They said I have to go get my laptop and start working from home."

"Really?" I asked in denial.

Todd nodded, lips pressed together under his salt and pepper mustache.

"When?"

"Immediately. The U.S. declared a national emergency." Todd returned the phone to his pocket, grabbed his work badge, and headed out the door to make the one minute drive to his office.

It was Todd's second call in two days of changes made due to the 2019 novel coronavirus outbreak, a contagious respiratory infection originating in mainland China. The previous day, March 12, 2020, the call came from PEMA, the Pennsylvania Emergency Management Agency, informing him they were activating as the disease struck the commonwealth the week prior. Todd was the PEMA representative for his employer, the Pennsylvania Turnpike Commission. It was his duty to give daily updates of any needs or operational changes the Turnpike made due to the pandemic.

Both calls were like a slap in the face. I had seen news coverage of precautions taken in the epicenter—facial coverings, social distancing, travel bans, quarantine—but I naively thought our country's excellent medical advancements would nip the virus in the bud well before it reached central PA. Also, I only, ignorantly, thought about the epidemic affecting our travel ability and was relieved since returning home to Dauphin County from our first trip to sunny California.

Todd had a work conference in Redwood City at the end of February, and for the price of my plane fare, I tagged along to one of my bucket list destinations. In hindsight, Todd should have tranquilized me and checked me with the luggage. The airport crowds and sardine-packed flights whacked my anxiety up to crippling status. I should have calmed myself with controlled breathing and EFT tapping, but I hadn't flown in 28 years and was distracted by wondering if the physics of flight were still in play.

I remained tense though the plane took off and landed in Atlanta without issue. My panic attack emerged during the connecting flight to San Francisco with the desperate urge to stand up and shout, "I've got to get out of here!" like the hysterical woman in the movie *Airplane*. I wished Leslie Nielsen was still alive to shake and slap me a few times. Alas, he was not, but I had Todd.

"Breathe, baby," he said, breaking into my manic thoughts.

I exhaled, not realizing I was holding my breath.

"It'll be okay," he said. "We'll get through this together." He clasped my hand in both of his and I relaxed from its warm security.

Todd dashed my hopes of meaningful eye contact when he whipped his head back to the window like a dog spotting a squirrel. According to our couples' therapist, we both had anxiety, as well as depression and other disorders, but Todd's exhibited itself differently than mine. Boy, howdy! When he wasn't enjoying the view or comforting me, Todd was his typical social butterfly-self making jokes and chatting with anyone who would listen. Meanwhile, I resumed my silent meltdown and searched for barf bags. I was horrified to find none.

My nerves, which relaxed once we exited the airport, pulled taut again like guitar strings as we dodged the crazy highway traffic. By the time we reached the hotel, I knew my fear would cage me the following day while Todd attended the conference. Yet, after a sound night's sleep, my resolve emerged. It also helped when Todd reminded me that I always wanted to come to California, and the local meteorologist proclaimed clear skies with record-high late February temperatures. The deciding factor was the news anchor announcing at least one person was in a California hospital with coronavirus symptoms, though there was no known infected contact nor international travel involved. Instead of diving beneath the covers as I expected, the news made me determined to see the Pacific Ocean. What if it was now or never? You can always turn back, I told myself, but you've got to try.

I set the vehicle's navigation for Half Moon Bay and white-knuckled it all the way. Elation eclipsed my worry when I turned into the parking lot and saw the ocean. I peeled my fingers from the steering wheel, grabbed my backpack and camera, and hiked the long path to the beach access. The morning haze had burned off and I stared in awe as the blue sky married the water.

I smiled and plopped my large rear down on the sand in my ill-suited long-sleeved shirt, jeans, and sneakers, for once not caring what anyone thought. I closed my eyes and inhaled the cleansing salt air. The crashing waves were like holy water on my mental demons. I felt empowered and I thanked God I made it there. I drove Todd there that evening and showed him the view proudly, as if to say, *here's the tranquil place that made me forget about my mental illness and the rat race of life.* As we stood in an embrace and watched the glowing sunset into the vast sea, I knew he felt the same.

It was hard to believe only fifteen days had passed. Since then, over one hundred thousand people were ill globally, including those stuck on cruise ships, schools and businesses closed, travel curtailed, and countries were on lockdown. By March 16th, San Francisco Bay area residents were ordered to shelter-in-place for weeks to halt the circulation of the virus. It was eerie imagining the wharf, our last California destination spot, silent save for the barks of the sea lions sunbathing at Pier 39. My vacation anxieties seemed silly in light of the invisible foe infecting, spreading, and killing like a cancer, an evil I knew all too well. Still, I continued in my denial, like I had as a teenager told my mother's disease was terminal.

The call I received in the early hours of March 25th forced me to face reality. My boss, at the municipal police station I clerked for, stated I was to "stay home until further notice." They would be operating with limited civilian staff to mitigate the spread. I choked on my anxiety, rising like bile. I was certain I'd continue working as the police department never closed. Without my daily routine, my fear quickly spiraled into a depressive funk. I reverted to my unhealthy way of self-soothing: television and junk food. If my therapist knew, she would say, "It looks like we may have regressed. Let's regroup and refocus on moving forward."

But I was stuck in the quicksand of my depression. I sunk further into the pit of despair when I realized I wouldn't see my dad for his 70th birthday on March 28th. Not immune-deficient like myself, but he was vulnerable to the virus due to age and having had a precancerous kidney removed recently. I wallowed for weeks until I had an epiphany: seclusion was nothing new to me. I was an awkward only child, who grew into an unpopular and angry teenager, then became a rebellious young adult with trust and abandonment issues, who then settled into a middle-aged homebody diagnosed with mental illness. Isolation was like an old comfortable coat I used to wear daily. Plus, I was getting paid to stay home, which was my dream come true!

Meanwhile, quarantine for Todd was a living nightmare. While I dove into my neglected crafts and spending time with our two Siberian huskies, he was drowning in overworked solitude. Todd was like Norm from *Cheers* without the bar, his stool, and his pals. By late April, with over 40,000 Pennsylvanians infected, we were under a stay-at-home order. It became too much for Todd and he lashed out like a caged wild animal.

"I can't take this!" Todd screamed. "I hate my job. I hate everything."

Focused on my own mental health, I had forgotten to check in on his.

He sobbed, which terrified me more than the global pandemic. Instead of waiting for another life-changing call to come, we made one for a much needed virtual therapy appointment. We couldn't and shouldn't handle this without assistance.

"Breathe, Sweetie." I wrapped my arms around him and promised, "It will be okay. We'll get through this together."

And we did, one day at a time.

Donna Leiss *is the author of three published short stories:* The Black Dress *in the anthology* Strange Magic, The Nine Lives of Squeekie *in the collection,* The Second and Third Nine Lives of Squeekie the Bookstore Cat, *and* The Princess Tower in The Very Very Bad Misadventures of Annika the Reluctant Bookstore Cat. *She is an alumnus of Elizabethtown College and a member of Penn Writers. Donna currently resides in Middletown, PA with her husband and two Siberian huskies who, despite their mother's stories, are very anti-cat.*

My Life with COVID-19

by Krystian Leonard

In March 2020, I was in the midst of a senior project at WVU, working with some great young women who had brilliant ideas for our project to surpass the grading scale and hopefully get published by 100 Days of Appalachia. We were ready to launch our interviews and even set dates to travel together in and out of the state to visit some music performance halls. Spring was around the corner, which meant so was spring break. Then our professor asked for a mandatory meeting with all the seniors and told us news that would change all of our plans. Meetings, interviews, and our projects would be postponed until further notice. We were told to go home, wherever that may be, and stay alert for emails concerning our projects. I received a call from a friend, urging me to stock up on any flu medication and necessities as soon as possible and head directly home until the news broke. COVID-19 would take over our projects and our future plans.

Going home that day I felt a real, terrifying fear. How serious would this disease be? Would it be in my hometown? How many people would I personally know be impacted by it? All of these questions swimming in my mind would be answered in a matter of weeks. I was furloughed from my waitressing job, my mother had to start working from home, and grocery store runs were so stressful we were left with barely enough supplies and sanity to make it through the week. This led to my family giving up on going to the grocery stores altogether and using services such as Instacart so we wouldn't have to be overly exposed to others. Even using a grocery service lead to us sanitize our bags of food and supplies on our front porch.

Taking shoes off in the garage and spraying them with disinfectant, removing clothes immediately in the laundry room and putting them in the wash, then taking a shower became the routine if any of us went anywhere outside our home. It even came down to the point of not allowing my boyfriend to come over at all and I would have to stay down with his family for days at a time if I wanted to see him at all. It was so scary and the uncertainty of who could catch the virus was extremely stressful. In the beginning, my mother and I would barely even hug each other because of the fear that one of us was carrying the disease and could possibly transmit it to the other one. I worried about my internship. I was hired in February and I dreamed of getting hired full time after the semester was over, but with this virus destroying jobs across the country, I had no idea if I would even last as an intern.

Every day, on every news channel, social media outlet, and more were all focused on COVID-19, there was no outrunning this ruthless disease. As the death tolls increased, my fear for loved ones went along with it. I had family members with underlying health conditions such as diabetes and heart disease. Every day I said a small prayer for protection over them. My heart broke every time I read a story about families losing loved ones and hospitals struggling to stay safe and still help those suffering from this virus. My aunt is a nurse and every time she was in contact with someone diagnosed with COVID-19, she let us know and my concern for her safety was at an all-time high.

As the days continued, so did the theories about how and why we were under attack from this deadly virus? Images from around the world showed so many people trapped in their homes fearing for their safety. Media outlets were relentlessly bombarding us 24 hours a day, social media was rampant with conspiracy theories, and so we hid. We stayed home, and then we started to gain focus on the things that were most valuable. Our families. I got busy with my internship, and then thankfully was offered a permanent position. How incredible to be offered this opportunity in a time when so many were experiencing great loss. My new job gave me greater focus and energy. I happily ordered a new desk online and set up shop in my room. Focusing on things I could control gave me a sense of stability. I eagerly worked and processed all of my new hire duties and celebrated by taking my dog, Ludo, out on beautiful long walks. Breathing in fresh air and telling myself everything would get better, it had to get better. I wanted to keep my job and now the fear and chatter that schools could be canceled indefinitely terrified me. What would our world look like without the current education system? Learning online could be such a challenge, I was a little jealous of the children who were sent home from school, it seemed like every child's dream, but a real nightmare for educators and parents.

Slowly but surely, we discovered our circle of friends and family, thankfully, did not have any Covid cases. And once our routines became established, a sense of new normal came into play. Ordering our groceries, cooking, walking, working, and then looking for projects to fill in the gaps, gave peace of mind. I am used to a busy travel schedule, and when all of my booked events were canceled, well, I was left with just me and my family and my sweet boyfriend. We spent those days really reflecting on what it means to be alive in this crazy time. My life had been somewhat sheltered from hardships. My family experienced 9-11, but I was so young I don't remember it. And here we were, living thru a global pandemic, wondering if we were going to get sick, or worse, make someone we love sick just by giving a hug, sharing a laugh, or having a meal together.

Every week we waited to hear what the next shortage would bring, so we restocked when we could. My special gluten-free diet meant I had to do without some items and my family spent days looking for meat until I found a local market and then started making weekly trips for eggs and beef products. Items we took for granted, made me step back and realize how fortunate I was. I miss my time in crowded restaurants and packed movie theaters. And I am already lamenting that Mom and I won't have our annual Black Friday shopping weekend. Fourth of July was different for me this year, as I braved an airplane ride to Florida, with mask and sanitizer galore. My boyfriend's family rented a beautiful beach home away from the crowds and we sat and rested and pretended things would be normal soon enough. Only to come home and endure another quarantine away from my family for two weeks, filled with temperature checks and a Covid 19 test to ensure I was not a carrier. I hope I am one of the lucky ones that will not be a carrier. I pray my family stays safe and healthy. And I look forward to the day when I wake up to hear news a vaccine or treatment has been found to end this nightmare. But until that happens, I will continue to work and live my life to the fullest extent possible.

Just last week, I learned my grandmother was exposed to a coworker who tested positive for Covid. So now we wait for test results to come back and pray again.

Krystian Leonard *is the award-winning author of Shining Scars, dedicated to helping children cope and embrace their visible scars. She is President and Founder of Shining S.C.A.R.S. 501(c)3, a nonprofit dedicated to helping children cope and embrace their visible scars. Tedx speaker, actress, pageant competitor. and a Zoom Into Books Author.*

Working in the Weeds

by Lynn Salsi

It was no surprise that university classes moved online. I heard it on the radio traffic station on March 11th as I drove home from class, "The Governor of Georgia will hold a press conference to discuss the pandemic." The next day at 4:45 p.m. the campus closed and students evacuated dormitories. Classes resumed online six days later.

It seems half a lifetime has passed.

With interruptions of familiar aspects of my life—not seeing students, no drives to campus, no friends to greet at church, and cancellation of book events, my days took on a foreign routine. Rules to shelter-in-place created the disruption, not because our family of three wanted "to be alone together," but because rules were imposed on all lives. What happened to our free country and would all the old people die?

Our little dog, Ossie's morning constitutional became a ritual. Mornings in a bathrobe offered a few minutes of reflection before going online. As I walked through the back yard looking at daffodils in bloom, I thought how I might turn the place into a *bona fide* garden with a pebble path like the one on YouTube. Two ancient gardenias covered with hundreds of buds seemed like a promise, but I crossed my fingers hoping frost was over. Ossie ran through emerging cone flowers and daisies planted ten years ago, stopping to sniff the scent of baby rabbits and their mother that lived in the overgrowth at the back fence. I looked for gerberas in places where I'd planted for two decades. They often freeze during cold months, with their re-appearance depending on nature rather than nurture. *This can become a cutting garden*, I mused, knowing I'd planned that since my children left home nine years ago.

I was vigilant about emerging gerberas and began weeding only after seeing tiny sharp-edged leaves break through the earth. To weed too early causes baby plants to be mistaken for weeds. I marked possible plants and pulled only identifiable weeds for two weeks. After that, I counted twenty returns. My mother might have said, "They are harbingers of spring."

Mid-March to early May meant hours online and texting with students ages 19 and 20 who never had studied online. I had coffee and Ossie's outing before answering 40 to 50 texts and dealing with writing due late March that took some students until early April to submit. Students booted from dorms and predictable lives moved home or isolated in apartments. They missed friends, freedom, and questioned government intrusion. None seemed depressed. Most were frustrated with rules that dictated their new unpredictable lives.

Many parents depended on their college-children to help younger siblings with online lessons. One student took care of his ten-year-old brother and his great grandmother suffering from Alzheimer's. Many with part-time jobs moved to fulltime. Some at Chick-Fil-A shared photos in real-time of two lines of cars encircling the building. "This is a mad-house," Kent wrote. "Everyone wants chicken. At this rate, I'll be able to pay tuition for the next two semesters. By the way, I'm begging for an extension for the paper due tomorrow." A student's dad died. He became the breadwinner and had two weeks to find a less expensive apartment. Bea, who could only afford two courses a semester, gave up a fry-cook job to chase her nursing dream. She earned a CMA last December and worked in a senior care home. She texted, "Professor, I saw a patient die. I feel numb, but I work again in an hour. How can I possibly finish my writing class? Help me!"

I had a few advantaged students, ones with credit cards, the latest mobile phone, and a cool car. Jenna texted an invitation to come to Acapulco. She found a "super-cheap" plane ticket, a five-star room for a one-star price, and her classroom became a beach in Mexico.

Regardless, 152 students kept streaming personal issues, more than questions about assignments. None were meant to be humorous. "I didn't sign up for this. Whoever thinks online education is a good thing is crazy. I'm applying for a refund. Can you spot me an extra 20 points on that paper? I deserve an A for putting up with this crap. I need a human. I'm too busy to study. I'm in home prison. My dad is a plumber, and I'm his new assistant. I have to go to work and can't be late."

My backyard became a refuge. It substituted for lunch off-campus, tea-parties with two granddaughters, and laughs with students who hung around after classes. But that bastion of sanity turned into a week of flooding April rain that brought weeds—fast growing, thick, pernicious, along with a total quarantine inside. When the sun reappeared, my husband offered a short-term rescue and helped weed, but I knew it wasn't his thing. I wondered if he thought it was my thing. With two weeks left in the semester and 1,500 final-exam essay pages to read and grade, yard-time became limited. Not wanting to lose momentum, I checked neighborhood online posts to see if any handy-kids wanted to earn money. Sixteen-year-olds asked $12.00 to $15.00 an hour. Weed tending immediately became "my thing" as I finished reading digital papers under the large red umbrella. Forced garden care gave me breaks that refreshed my mind after fifty pages or so.

Late papers added to final grading drudgery the fourth week in April. I mustered patience and headed toward the finish-line of averaging grades. By then there were rewards some mornings as I returned inside with handfuls of flowers. Daily relaxation came in the dirt beds where I realized I was thinking my own thoughts. With no one to interfere, I freshened my brain for the last few papers I had to grade. As I saw my garden come to life, I thought about my dad. He had a green thumb—an amazing one. I thought how, in childhood, I followed him down camellia-lined paths in February and early March. Camelias were his pride. Neighbors came on Sunday afternoons to admire blooms—the same ones that won him prizes at the annual Camelia Show. The day before guest arrivals, he paid ten-year-old me a quarter to pick up dead blossoms on the ground. He was no push-over. I had to gather more than 50 to be paid. As I mulched, I wished I'd learned everything he wanted to teach me.

Re-entering the house took me back to questions, stressing students, reading assignments, and texts. But I was released from the misery when I posted semester grades. Finally, I sat and stared at the yard—assessing. Thirty years in one house meant thirty-years digging the same dirt. The impatiens I planted under the shade tree near the kitchen window formed magnificent pink mounds for 15 years before the tree died along with the one next to the garage where my two youngest sons played on a brightly-colored swing-set—orange, yellow, and red. A former neighbor—a curmudgeon, my mother called a "killjoy," told my husband to get rid of the plastic he declared tacky. He hated seeing it from his second-story bedroom window. Back then, I stifled the urge to add something more obnoxious.

By mid-May flower beds bloomed, tomatoes and peppers grew tall, bees and butterflies swarmed salvia and buddleia. Photos of beautiful day lilies were sent to my cousin who gave me the plant. After five weeks, blooming stopped and will not resume until next summer. The rabbits moved on to the park for better food, but a deer ate all the lilies in the front yard.

"You've taken on a lot," a neighbor said last week, as I observed the missing plants and the remains of our old post lamp bombed by bored teenagers who invaded our yard on the Fourth of July. "It's like the tomato that ate Cleveland," she said while picking up M-80 wrappers on the driveway. "How will you keep your complicated new landscape up?"

That conversation came before my husband put up another umbrella to keep me out of the sun during near-daily weeding because it gets hot after 9:00 a.m. Then last night I thought how the weeding might take another two summers and still, there was no pebble walkway. It had looked easy in the eight-minute video.

I had a fleeting thought that concrete covering the yard may have been best.

I've persisted, and my husband has become supportive of my vision. I now leave uprooted weeds stacked on the ground, and he throws them in the waste can. For Mother's Day, he bought me the King of Spades, a shovel with straight sharp edges that cut through heavy clay, making weeding easier. Now, in the evenings of late July, I say, "Bring me the King." Afterward, my husband sits under an umbrella and watches me dig weeds to create a proper new bed near the back fence.

Award-winning author, **Lynn Salsi** *is a Pulitzer Prize Nominee for her Appalachian Jack Tales series and is the author 29 books. She is a university professor and resides in Greensboro, NC. Lynn Salsi is a Zoom Into Books Author.*

Blessed and Disappointed

by Dennis Hetzel

Those are the two words that come to mind as I join millions of other Americans trying to make sense out of what the heck has happened in our country since March.

Blessed? That's me. When I dive into darker places in my head, I remind myself of that.

I get to spend most days in shorts and T-shirts, basking in the benefits of a life of hard work and a bit of luck assisted by my white-male privilege. My wife and I have enough resources, at least so far, to live at the beach (Holden Beach, North Carolina), where I can spend as much or as little time as I want with my writing, editing, and consulting work. I walk on the beach or ride my bike almost every day. I've had time to get better on guitar and do projects around the house and yard.

I've always been impatient; someone who looks down the road, feeling the pressure of the things I want to do and need to do, instead of living in the moment. Some of it follows naturally from decades of high-stress jobs and the other challenges of life. A lot of it goes to my inner demons – it's my nature to fear that things might not go well.

The precious gift of available time has been my revelation. Projects have become more manageable and even fun. My blood pressure is even lower.

Last week, I tried to repair my bike after a tube failure. Then the new tube failed, audibly leaking air. Former Dennis would have sworn, kicked the tire, and probably paid someone to do the repair at that point. This Dennis said, "hmm," expressed brief frustration, never lost his temper, did some online homework, figured out the problem, and sent away for the rim tape that should fix things.

We're healthy. We've stayed busy. We've binge-watched a lot of good television. We miss travel, dining out, and going to movies. We miss Friday night wine tastings. We won't be going on our cruise-of-a-lifetime to Europe in the fall. I know a few people who either have Covid or have loved ones with Covid, but, at least so far, we know no one who has died from it.

Our three adult children have stayed healthy and remain working and contributing. We miss seeing them, but we're scattered around the country. My daughter-in-law-to-be lost her job but found a replacement job, ironically helping unemployed Floridians navigating the on-purpose maze that is that state's unemployment system.

So, we're blessed.

That's obviously not true for millions of other people. I've done a little bit to help, surely not enough. As a member of my local Rotary Club in Shallotte, NC, I'm proud that we've supported the local food bank and other causes. As part of the praise team at Sharon United Methodist Church, I hope our musicians bring some thoughtful joy as we play to an audience on Facebook Live and a socially distanced, in-person congregation.

Meanwhile, since we live in a beach resort community, it's no surprise that Covid cases started exploding from next-to-nothing to nearly 1,000 in Brunswick County NC at this writing once the communities reopened and visitors began pouring in from across the East Coast and Midwest. The local economy wants and needs visitors. No one denies that.

Still, that brings me to disappointment.

Fast forward to Spring 2020.

My wife and I decide to get takeout food from the Provision Company, our favorite local restaurant. I go to pick up the food. I see a few signs posted about takeout and seating, but there's no effective system. I am one of the very few wearing a mask, standing elbow to elbow around the counter with people either waiting for tables, waiting for takeout orders, or leaving and trying to pay.

Sadly, this is an oft-repeated scene around the country. Compared to what Americans accomplished during World War II, our sacrifice requests are laughingly minimal to get the pandemic under control. We are asked to wear masks in situations where we can't socially distance. We are asked to avoid large groups, particularly indoors. We are asked to wash our hands frequently. We are asked to stay home with just family members as much as we can.

My wife and I try to stay safe and try to keep others safe. We have driveway "happy hours" with a few friends these days and support local businesses that are taking the safety of their customers and employees seriously.

We're disappointed to see so many Americans around us and across the country who refuse to do these simple, obvious things to protect themselves and others and help our economy get back on track faster.

As Americans, we're all blessed. I think we can do better. That certainly includes me.

Dennis Hetzel *has written two award-winning political thrillers,* Killing the Curse *and* Season of Lies and *his recent book,* The Vanished. *You'll find his book reviews regularly at BookTrib.com. Learn more at DennisHetzel.com. Dennis Hetzel is a Zoom Into Books Author.*

Pocket of Peace

by Stacie Haas

The day was June 12, 2020. I had squeezed my backside into a faded green rubber seat and held tight to rusty metal chains with both hands. Muscle memory I'd developed in childhood kicked in and I swung like I didn't have a care in the world. That was quite a feat considering the world was, at that moment, burning in protest against the murder of a black man by a white cop and one that had my parents hunkering down in fear of an invisible pandemic-causing virus.

I've conjured heaven many times, but swinging there, I wondered why it hadn't ever materialized as a playground. The temperature was hovering around 80 degrees, the sun slowly descending into the treetops at half-past eight o'clock. A slight breeze teased my skin in just the right way—not too warm like the sticky air that hangs in August or the cool spring winds that cause goosebumps. Aside from perfect weather, I'd also had the perfect view. My oldest son, Tom, was playing with his two-year-old brother, Joey. Tom followed Joe up the wooden fort and back down again, supported him on the jungle gym so he could climb like his hero, Spiderman, and pushed him on the toddler swing, drawing out his sweet laughs…those unmistakable, smile-inducing giggles that only babies are capable of producing and no adult is immune from.

My often-moody teenager was giving me a moments' reprieve, allowing me to swing as I once had on the public schoolyard of my youth. That play area was oddly similar to where I sat. Directly in front of me was a hot metal slide with a tall ladder and small guard rail. The ground was covered in gravel and two climbing structures that tempted falls and broken bones beckoned from the right, just in front of a wooden fort with a fireman's climbing pole. I was amazed that I wasn't worried. I didn't wish for a plastic tube slide, rubber tire floor, or the hand sanitizing stations featured in modern-day parks. Since I'd been paralyzed in fear of simply leaving my house for months, these dangers seemed like, dare I say, child's play.

We sat on a waitlist for years before gaining membership at the game and fish association in Kentucky, our home state, that built the playground. There we have a permanent campsite for our Jayco popup that overlooks the water. Mike, my husband of nearly 20 years, calls it his happy place. I was never as enamored as he, but I considered changing my mind while swaying on that swing. I turned my head in the direction of that second home of his, where he and our other son and seven-year-old daughter were fishing for crappie but were likely hooking baby bluegill.

What would my colleagues at the Fortune 500 I work for say about this place? I'd spent the better part of the previous three weeks crafting statements against racism, commiserating with my African American friends about their pain, and figuring out how our company could make things better for our black employees and customers. As a diverse person myself—half Chinese and looking every bit of it—I understood why these things were necessary. As a public relations professional, it was my job to protect the company's reputation. But part of me felt like a fraud for staying silent as the conversations spun beyond the world of work and into politics.

I often get pulled into discussions involving liberal values because colleagues presume my minority status means I have a sympathetic ear. Maybe I do, maybe I don't, but I'm dismayed by their assumptions. Aren't we supposed to stop pre-judging people based on ethnicity? Isn't that prejudice, too? I wonder what they'd say if they knew my pro-God, pro-life positions often caused me to vote the other way.

Sometimes I feel a primordial urge to share more of who I am, but it's a big risk with little return. I shouldn't have to prove my stance against racism, but if I suggest that we aren't as divided as the media suggests, then my non-whiteness, my African-American family members, and my authorship of an award-winning multicultural book are simply not enough. Colleagues already have an inkling that I'm not quite as open as they think, but they never ask. That way, they can stay in their bubble, and so can I.

Even the COVID-19 pandemic has turned political. Some on the right say the need for the economic lockdown was a scam; on the left, they say the president is going to kill people when he resumes campaign rallies. Of course, the mass gatherings for protests were apparently safe. For our national health experts, social justice suddenly became more important than social distancing. My mind spins thinking about all of it, and that's why swinging like a kid at the club was preferable overthinking at all.

Did I find it ironic to feel such peace there…in a place where it wouldn't surprise to see a Confederate flag flown from a truck bed? I've never seen one, but then again, it wouldn't offend me. As a student of Civil War history and having once dated a guy who did fly one, I get that it signifies a rebel spirit more than it does racism—if it means that at all. I abhor the lack of history being taught nowadays and have to wonder if the rioters tearing down our statues understand anything, including the nuances of the conflict or the fact that 600,000 people died in a war that expanded freedom.

I wouldn't have begrudged anyone for wondering if the predominantly white male club membership would frown upon a diverse crowd. I once worried about it, too, but it proved unnecessary. The club folks are the most genuinely kind-hearted people you'll ever meet. Very few are what you'd call wealthy or privileged, and many grew up quite poor in rough, tough Newport along the Ohio River. Many have diverse families like mine. Some have grandkids in jail for drug offenses or worse. And nearly all of them would give you the shirt off their back if you needed it.

Shotgun fire is a normal sound at the club, booming out in rapid succession, and that day was no exception. It, along with the earthiness and manliness of the place, comforted me in a world I no longer understood. The shots didn't drown out the birds, or the breeze, or my beautiful boys enjoying each other; they complemented it. I'm no good with a shotgun, but this little half-Chinese girl whose height is just five feet can make a mess of a Coke can with her .32 police special. There's safety in following God's commandments, safety in respecting law and order, and safety in knowing how to defend yourself—just as there's safety from Covid-19 if you can social distance, wash your hands often, and can avoid touching your face.

Peace on a playground swing. I wasn't about to surrender it for anything, not civil unrest, a pandemic, or politics. The virus had been dogged in its attempts to take my peace away. Lockdowns and "healthy at home" mandates stole our spring and threatened our summer. It took away my kids' social life and sports seasons and normal school days. It robbed us of our birthday celebrations, our pool days, our summer vacation. Most devastating, it pilfered the fragile defenses I maintained to protect me from the fact that life could go on without my parents in our daily lives. But I didn't think of that, not while I was on the swing.

Feeling the wind in my hair quieted the conflicts in my heart, the questions for which I had no answer. I didn't mourn the loss of 117,000 Americans, the Holy Eucharist, or baseball while in motion, nor did I try to solve the racial tension in the country. I didn't think about the autonomous zone in Seattle, the toppling of our nation's historical monuments, or President Trump's tweets.

So I pushed higher and higher, to the point where my insides did flip flops like when my dad drove fast over the hills and valleys of John Gray Road in Cincinnati when I was a kid. My brothers and I used to call that stretch of road the yahoo hill before development flattened it. I felt yahoo hill-type butterflies as I reached new heights. I wondered if I should jump off the swing like I used to when I was a light-hearted girl, long before life got complicated. Did I dare?

In the end, the pocket of peace I'd found was enough. I just kept swinging.

Stacie Haas *is the author of* Freedom for Me: A Chinese Yankee, *winner of the Literary Classics gold medal for Coming of Age Upper Middle Grade fiction in 2018. She resides with her husband and their four children in the Commonwealth of Kentucky. Find her at StacieHaas.com.*

Covid and Cancer

by Ellen M. Still

As I write this, the Covid pandemic is raging in the United States, my state is a hot spot, and I am undergoing treatment for breast cancer.

My personal Covid 19 stay at home order came a little earlier than for most. Covid was not a big worry for many on February 14, but I had to take extra precautions because I celebrated this Valentine's Day with a double mastectomy. This was the second time breast cancer had visited me and this time, my journey required visits to chemotherapy land and radiation island.

Now being the self-centered person I am, I figured if I had to be ill, I might as well take advantage of the situation. I planned to plead, entreat, and guilt my friends into cookies, cakes, pies, and free lunches. And perhaps a flower and plant or two, maybe five or six. Instead, I was isolated early and put in a distinct, but caring bubble.

Thanks to the pandemic, I had to face my chemotherapy treatments alone. These procedures take about five to six hours and you just sit there while anti-nausea drugs, killer cell drugs, and other lovely things get fed into your veins. It is boring. Even books lose their ability to entertain after a while. Before Covid, friends could visit, play cards, or just gossip. Spouses brought lunch or just sat and kept you company. Not so with the pandemic. The entire visit to chemo land, beginning with entering the medical facility to walking out seemingly eons later, had to be done solo. At least someone drove me.

Solo was also pretty much the way I faced my downtime. This is the time you have no energy, you can only sit and wait while the one or two weeks to pass until your fatigue is improved, but then you undergo another chemo session, and the whole thing starts over again. As the Covid impact grew, many friends began staying home themselves and while they were concerned somewhat about visiting me before, now they were terrified. It was as if a wall suddenly grew between me and all those I knew and cared about. It is not that people quit caring about me. People were afraid to bring food because the experts had not determined if the virus was transmitted that way. So no cookies, cakes, or lunches. Then too, when everything is shut down, it is a little hard for someone to send flowers or pick up basil salmon over fried rice. Thank goodness a few friends had stocked up on encouraging cards or made their own and kept the US post office busy.

Perhaps one of the most difficult times during the pandemic was when my hair began to fall out. It was not the fact I would be bald either. Since the beauty shops were closed and friends obeyed the stay at home order, who was available to shave my head? My husband. It is one thing for you to know your loved one has a possibly deadly disease; it is quite another to have to remove a part of that beloved's physical appearance. He dealt with it, but it wasn't easy. He tried to cover up his realization that this was really, really happening, and did a pretty good job of it. But I knew. I think it was easier for him to get used to looking at a wife who resembles a combination of Tweety Bird and Bruce Willis. As for me? I keep wondering who the heck that woman in the mirror is. My hair is now a whole half-inch long, so when I go out in the ninety-degree heat without a head covering, I tell myself I'm making a fashion statement. At least no one has run screaming into the night when they saw me. It is much, much too hot here to cover up with a cap or a wig.

Several people told me I was fortunate that everyone had to stay at home, which meant I had lots of company. But let me say that being ill and isolated from friends, family, church, familiar places, and activities is an entirely different matter. I talked with several fellow cancer patients and they all described the same feelings of double isolation. Calls, texts, and cards became a lifeline – but a somewhat sterile one. It warms my heart when a friend remembers my situation in any way, but what I really wanted, still want, is a heartfelt hug. Perhaps in that neediness, I am no different from anyone else during this pandemic. Elbow bumping is just not the same.

On the upside, friends I had not talked with in years heard about my diagnosis and contacted me to let me know they were sending good vibes my way. It was encouraging to hear from them, one from as far away as upstate New York and another from Dublin, Ireland. It was a delight when a couple of friends I thought of as casual ones became mainstays. There was one downside, however. Individuals and colleagues I thought of as caring simply disappeared into the woodwork, or called once, early on and in my weakened state that hurt terribly. But then it probably serves me right. I might have been one of those in the past, but I have learned my lesson, I hope.

As the pandemic means we are all stuck at home, more or less, the televisions are humming more than ever, at least at my house. Have you ever noticed that when anyone dies in TV dramas or movies, it is almost always from cancer? I never noticed that fact before. Frankly, it doesn't bother me, but I wondered if it gave my husband a jolt. To learn the answer, for myself and for you, dear reader, I asked him. His response? "Not anymore."

My pandemic cancer life remains an absolute whirlwind of visits to the oncologist, trips to physical therapy, meetings with the radiologist, and conversations with nurses. Nevertheless, I envy those who get to go grocery shopping or trek to the drug store. "Really?" you ask. It's very true. While my husband, God love him, is acting as my personal shopper, I continue to suffer from withdrawal due to the lack of opportunity to say to a salesperson, "I'm just looking." I long to search for a dress, check out the decorative pillows, or even have the chance to pick out fresh peaches and corn. Now that sounds pretty desperate, but that's how I feel. My area is a hot spot, so no shopping trips for me.

Friends are very concerned about my trips to radiation island, worried that the medical facility is a breeding ground for Covid. Sadly, but fortunately, the cancer facility is probably one of the safest places for me. There I can be sure everyone wears a mask, social distances, and washes their hands. There has been no mask mandate from the governor in this state and it was one of the first to reopen. The mask user rate here remains one of the lowest in the nation. Never mind the 17 percent positive test rate day after day. This lack of protection from others is especially dangerous for me, given my lowered immune system.

To those who say wearing a mask takes away their freedom, I say your stance takes away MY freedom to shop, eat out, visit with friends, work at my job. In this nation, there are laws that prohibit you from yelling "fire" in a theatre and ones that require you to wear a seat belt. Is requiring a mask so different? Many of our laws, regulations, and rules concern "the public good," and no one marches in the streets or honks horns arguing those laws take away their independence or step on their constitutional rights. By the way, I don't like masks either, but they save lives. They might save mine.

Yes, the isolation can be spirit dampening, to say the least, but unlike others I know, I have been spared the worst of the pandemic so far. I have a cousin who manages a hospital's radiation department. She called us crying after we sent her N-95 masks and a face shield. They were running so dangerously low at her hospital; the staff was ordered to use the same mask for three days or more. My physical therapist volunteered to oversee staff in the Covid ward as they suited up to ensure their protective gear was on properly to reduce the chance of infections. She still cannot talk about her experiences.

Me? My fatigue is gone. I haven't caught Covid (fingers crossed); only one friend has had the virus and that was a mild case. My eyebrows and eyelashes are back – mostly. I had a long weekend at a friend's vacation home in the mountains. My husband and I both have our jobs. I have a spouse who, after "house arrest" and this illness, remains fascinating. I get to watch the cardinals and bluebirds at the feeders. Life is good.

The Wacky Side of Danger

by Joyce W. Nissley

Meeting Phil was risky. The news media carried reports of danger. "The Virus is still out there!" officials warned. "Wear a mask. Stay six feet apart." Online dating could also be dangerous. "Don't do it," my sister warned.

As I drove with determination in my Swedish wagon, glancing periodically at the clock, and concerned about being too late, I was thinking even more about being an exemplary citizen through twelve weeks of complying with stay-at-home orders. I had been dutiful because I worried about becoming infected by this dreaded Covid-19 and thereby transmitting to my family and staff or my newfound retirement friends. That would have made me a hated person, whereas being loved was my preference. Now I was ready to relax a bit under new rules of openness.

As I pulled into the tree-lined lot, I considered that I was ready, as ready as possible under the circumstances. I had my mask, my wallet, and lipstick. I was well-rested and armed with several witty remarks if needed. My biggest challenge would be not to break down in tears. Stress can do that, although rarely.

We had agreed to an early dinner on the patio at El Serrano, not far from where I lived, but a 45-minute drive for Phil. I parked beside the building, put on my mask, and walked to the back of the building, where I expected to find the patio and/or Phil. I was glad to see a large Entrance sign but no sight of Phil. I proceeded into the patio, which turned out to be a beautiful grand courtyard with Peruvian styling. A few people were seated, but not Phil.

"How many are in your party?" the hostess asked. She was sitting at the end of a short counter, leaning slightly over the tablet of names, with her long pretty hair falling gently forward.

"Just two," I said. "I thought you might require a reservation."

"It's not necessary," she said. I could picture her smile, hidden by her mask. Her manner was accepting, not indifferent, as might be expected if resentful for the mostly empty tables.

I decided to wait outside near the Entrance sign, where I found a selection of rustic wooden benches. I chose the one that was partly shaded. This was a perfect day, June 16, 2020, to be exact, with very warm sun and cool breeze, my favorite weather. My face was in the sun, but the mask was covering my nose, in need of protection. My dermatologist would be happy.

I was content to be outdoors where the sun-averse Virus does not lurk as readily. I was glad I had worn jeans, clean and well pressed. Maybe my top was not the perfect choice, though. With bell-shaped sleeves starting at the elbow, it was lovely, and it was expensive. I should be cautious about the splintering wood against my back. Although I was not keeping score exactly, I would need to evaluate all aspects of the evening carefully at the end.

I began to grow a bit restless, tired of watching a mostly empty parking lot and wondering what might have happened to Phil when a black sedan came into view and parked at the far end of the lot. A tall impressive man with grey hair and grey mustache appeared from the car and walked slowly toward me. I waved, and so did he. This was Phil, a stranger, except for a few brief messages online and an hour-long phone call yesterday. This was the man who could be the love of my life or break my heart or any number of wild scenarios that I did not want to consider and improper to mention here. He was holding a mask in his hand.

We introduced ourselves, avoiding a handshake or hug because this was the new normal way of being friendly, which equated to being just the opposite.

The hostess kindly showed us to a shady table, which we requested. I chose a chair, and Phil sat beside me. I was about to suggest making more distance between us when he actually moved his chair closer to me. This simple action could cost me my life, but I was more interested in his blue eyes and willing smile. I removed my mask, as allowed when seated.

"We could order a bottle of wine," Phil suggested.

"Ordinarily, I would love to share that with you, but I stopped drinking wine," I said, wondering whether I had told him during the lengthy phone call.

"I would like to have lemonade," I said when the waiter asked. Disappointed that it was not available, I ordered club soda instead. Phil had the same.

Phil said, "So you own a winery, but you don't drink wine."

"I believe that I was drinking too much because our wine is too good. My last two sips were on January 1, 2017."

I could have continued telling the story, but we had a lot of ground to cover. This was something like a job interview. The goal was to present your best, fascinating self, without giving away anything that could disqualify you, meanwhile learning the other person's life history, listening for red flags and avoiding the distractions of personality and charm. On top of it all, the music was loud, so we needed to talk loudly, which is a risk factor for transmitting the virus, especially troublesome where either person is unknowingly asymptomatic, like now.

"I'm trying to figure you out," he said, leaning back. "I'm a realtor, and I learned to read people fast, but I'm not sure about you."

"That might be because I'm an introvert acting like an extrovert. I learned recently that I can be happier that way. However, unlike a true extrovert, the result is not just happiness but exhaustion."

He leaned close to my face, to speak confidentially. "I'm an introvert, too."

"Are you exhausted, like me?" I replied, hopefully.

"No," he admitted. Then he added, "You're cute."

We were mid-way in eating the fajitas that we ordered, and

I remembered part of the phone conversation when Phil said he did not drink much but liked a glass of wine with dinner. We decided to order one for him, and the waiter placed it beside me.

Phil invited me to taste it.

"No, thanks," I shook my head and moved the glass over to him.

He gently pushed the glass back toward me, and with his face close to mine, he said with charm, "Go ahead, a sip or two won't hurt."

A loud alarm went off in my head. "Listen. You have blue eyes, and I'm beginning to think you're the blue-eyed devil," I said, scaring even myself.

"My eyes are grey," he said.

I swallowed a bite of comforting refried beans. "I must admit, this is hard for me because you have a strong personality. You do bring out my comic side, though, and I like that."

He disagreed about his personality and resumed telling me about his life, like singing in his church choir as well as marrying and divorcing the soprano. I was listening intently.

"You seem more open now. I can see it in your face," he said.

"Compared to what? Do you mean when we met at the entrance?"

"Yes, you seemed uptight at the beginning."

"I was wearing a mask!" I blurted, and we both had to laugh.

Phil quickly began to tell me about dog training and how he found his current dog, a German shorthair pointer.

"Can your dog read?" I asked.

"She shakes her head back and forth, but I doubt she can read," he said.

"I knew a dog who could read, and I wrote a story about that. May I send you the story?"

"I'd like that." He looked at me suspiciously.

"My next story is about a man I hired and fired due to an altercation, and — "

"What!! Altercation!!" he burst into laughter. "Who uses words like that?"

His reaction to the word hit me like the funniest thing I had ever heard, and instantly I was attacked by a laughing fit when your face goes into contortions and you can hardly breathe. Worst of all, you also lose bladder control. If I had been concerned earlier about crying, now I was really in trouble, but able to put the brakes on just in time.

"Sorry for the laughing fit," I said. "My twin is the only other person who triggers it."

"I talk too much," he offered. "Tell me about your twin. Are you identical?"

I talked for a while, and he continued to drink his wine at a snail's pace. After two hours, the interview was winding down.

As the evening came to a close in the parking lot, saying goodbye was difficult. I was unsure that I should continue to see this man who intrigued me. Wackiness aside, the virus and the man could adversely determine my own new normal. I could very possibly turn into a crushed online dating casualty, if not also a sorry Covid-19 victim.

Joyce Nissley *became interested in writing while a college freshman,when a story about childhood drew praise from her English instructor. Although she earned a B.A. Degree in English Literature, her career was primarily centered on her family's winery, established in 1976. Now retired, she is working on a collection of stories which will chronicle situations and characters associated with her career.*

Covid-19 Circle of Death?

by Warren Clark

A group of us neighbors started meeting, appropriately distanced from each other of course, on a neighbor's driveway in mid-March shortly after a Covid-19 shut-down was ordered for our neighborhood. This driveway was chosen because of a huge crepe myrtle tree that was strategically placed to shade us from the late afternoon sun. Back in March, the weather was quite pleasant, so we were just seeking shelter from the direct sun. Now, in mid-July, we have added fans, cold drinks, and much cooler clothing.

Mostly we get together for about an hour and a half in the late afternoon to share each other's company and to talk, with great wisdom, about any subject that comes up. Our discussions range from the mundane to the silly, to the truly bizarre. TV shows and movies are discussed at great length. We share stories from our childhood and early married life, with plenty of comic relief, which we find much more productive and uplifting than the constant din of gloom and doom from the media and politicians.

One of our favorite subjects is food. We discuss food preparation successes and failures, review restaurants that were visited many months ago, and exchange recipes. Sometimes someone will bring a home-cooked treat, which we all rave about, making sure that the treats don't stop coming. One couple brings a bag of fun-size chocolate candy to distribute to the group most afternoons, even when they can't stay for the conversation. We call them M&M but not for the reason you might think (sorry, that's an inside joke).

We also make a point of waving to every car that passes. Even those group members with their backs to the street throw up their hands. Most of the time, we get a wave and a smile back.

We sometimes complain about our children not calling us enough or calling us too much (the word 'meddling' has been mentioned once or twice). But there is never any doubt that we love our kids to death. One of them even gave us the nickname "Circle of Death" because she wasn't sure that her parents should be joining us. We have since won her over with our charm and impeccable manners. We even talked about having T-shirts made up for the group.

However, we never forget the serious economic impact and horror of the sickness and death that this pandemic has brought with it. It seems like nothing good could possibly come from something as horrific as this, but in our case, it has turned a group of friendly neighbors into a group of friends. "Circle of Death," indeed! I think we should be called the "Circle of Joy, Hope, and Comfort Under Extreme Circumstances," but all that would never fit nicely on a T-shirt!

Covid Memoir

by Lew Dobbins

Covid-19 has taken a huge bite out of my lust for living. I have been a part of live musical entertainment all of my adult life. Now, because of this hateful disease, the live performances are gone.

I miss the excitement of live entertainment expression. Since 1966 I have been involved with hundreds of live shows. Although I still maintain a part-time radio show, the CD's do not replace live entertainment.

I miss the Sagebrush Roundup, a live country music program, indoors every Saturday night on Bunner Ridge in Marion County. It is sad but true, traditional live country music at this time is dead.

Personally, I wear the mask and keep my distance. When I do go out, my visit has to be planned. We take so much for granted till something like this pandemic hits close to home.

May God bless the entertainer, and hopefully, for you and me, the live music will be re-structured sooner than later.

Lew Dobbins *is a member of the West Virginia Broadcasters and Country Music Halls of Fame. He is also an award-wnning author of the book,* Behind the Microphone, *a recounting of an illustrious career in country music, radio and TV. Lew Dobbins writes a personal history of country music and engages the reader with personal and professional stories of our country's greatest stars. Lew is a Zoom Into Books Author.*

Corona Chronicles

by Dreama Denver

Who could have imagined what the year 2020 would bring? As we rang in the New Year at midnight on January 1, we were celebrating what we thought would be the year of clarity, the year of perfect vision. 2020 had such a beautiful ring to it, not to mention how perfect it looked visually when written out. Sadly, 2020 would prove to be the most confusing, divisive, difficult year in my memory.

Who could have imagined terms like social distancing, flattening the curve, lockdown, herd immunity, quarantine, and pandemic becoming part of our daily narrative? Maybe we should have suspected that 2020 had it in for us when January alone saw so many disturbing events – the first case of something called COVID-19 reported in the state of Washington, the announcement of Prince Harry and Meghan Markle stepping away from the royal family, the shocking death of Kobe Bryant, his 13-year-old daughter Gigi, and seven others in a helicopter crash in California, and the horrifying wildfires in Australia – all during January.

Who could have imagined that by March, the entire world would be in lockdown? LOCKDOWN! Told to shelter in place, we were only allowed to venture outside the confines of our own little world for essentials like groceries and prescriptions, all the while wearing a mask, staying 6 feet apart, and using hand sanitizer when we couldn't wash our hands repeatedly. Good hygiene definitely made sense, but what didn't make sense to anyone was the run on toilet paper. For months it was impossible to find and that scarcity provided a touch of humor in the early days of quarantine.

Who could have imagined not being able to visit our loved ones in nursing homes or hospitals? For the families who lost loved ones during this pandemic, no funerals were allowed, which meant their loved ones died and were laid to rest alone. I lost my 92-year-old mother on January 29th just before the lockdown occurred and have been thankful every day since for the blessing of being able to be with her when she passed. Large gatherings of any kind were put on hold - no concerts, no church, no school, and no sporting events. The only large gatherings that seemed permissible were protests, some peaceful, some not-so-peaceful, some with protestors wearing masks and some with mask-less protestors screaming into each other's faces. Obviously, the mask requirement became very confusing, changing hourly and seemingly dependent on exactly what you were doing when you were or weren't wearing one. The frustration caused by this confusion sparked pro and con outrage all over social media. But even though confusion reigned, there were many blessings in the midst of the trials and that's what I'd like to focus on when it comes to my personal journey through this extraordinary time.

As a first-time children's book author, I was ecstatic about the official launch of my award-winning children's book, *Four Bears in a Box* set to take place at the Texas Library Association Conference in Houston at the end of March. Then came word the event was canceled due to Covid-19. In a matter of weeks, maybe even days, my appearance in Chicago at the American Library Association National Conference scheduled for June was also canceled. My book was about four bears *inside* their magical box, but my manager Burke Allen, my publisher Headline Books, and I were forced (like everyone else) to think *outside* the box for some magical way to promote my new release. Commonplace today, Facebook Live wasn't an everyday occurrence for most of us in March of 2020, but they became an almost hourly occurrence as authors, musicians, actors, and artists searched for ways to promote and entertain.

It's all in the timing! Isn't that what they say? The original version of *Four Bears in a Box* was written 20 years before. My husband, Bob Denver, better known to fans as Gilligan, had challenged me to write a children's book for our autistic son. He gave me a title, encouraged me to think 'Dr. Seuss' because our son loved his books so much and told me he had no doubt I could do it! So, I did it. I wrote the story in rhyme ala Dr. Seuss, and for my effort, got a big thumbs up from both Bob and Colin. Then, as often happens, life got in the way. Our son got older and more of a challenge to his parents, who provided his 24/7/365 care and, of course, my husband became ill and passed away. Through all those valleys, the bears were put away and forgotten. Then came the spring of 2019 when during a spring cleaning 'urge to purge' and I ran across my typewritten pages. An excited call to my manager resulted in a wonderful publisher in Headline Books, a topnotch illustrator in the enormously talented Ashley Belote, revisions that 20 years later made the book even timelier and a spring 2020 release date.

My book release on Facebook Live was a direct result of the country being quarantined and quarantine meant children were no longer in school; parents were forced to homeschool via the internet and, unexpectedly, families were sheltering in place 24 hours a day, spending every waking moment together. As the weeks went by, families became desperate for entertainment, diversion, anything to break the monotony. Enter my talented friend, actor Kevin Sizemore, who like the rest of us, was quarantined at home with his wife Gina and son Gunnar. Normally, Kevin would have been on location filming, but lockdown meant he was housebound, and, like all artists, looking for creative outlets. After my Facebook Live launch, Kevin called me.

"I want to do something with *Four Bears in a Box*, he told me. "I'm not sure exactly what, but I'm calling to ask if that would be okay with you."

Would that be okay with me?!? *Would that be okay??* Knowing Kevin's talent and determination, my answer was a resounding YES!

In a matter of weeks, the most endearing video of my book was launched on YouTube. Produced by Kevin, read by Charlie Adler—the voice of *Tiny Toons'* Buster Bunny, the director of "Kung Fu Panda," one of the top voice actors in the business and with music provided by Nashville singer/songwriter and beautiful friend, Delnora Reed, the video brought my book to life in a way I never imagined. Three crazy-talented artists used their time in quarantine to create something magical for isolated children and parents everywhere. And they did it with my children's story! In this case, it was 'all in the timing.'

There's nothing like quarantine to make you stop or at least slowdown and take stock of your life.

I stopped, and in a way I hadn't before, grasped how fragile our freedom is. I've worked with veterans for over a decade and those relationships have shown me that freedom certainly isn't free, but lockdown gave all of us a taste of what it would be like to lose our freedoms completely. We can never let happen. Too many have fought and died to make this country a beacon of hope to people all over the world.

I slowed down and looked around at the beauty of God's creation. All this mad-dashing through life makes us miss so much. How often do we *not* notice an awe-inspiring cloud formation, a sunrise or sunset, the peacefulness of a solitary walk? Henry David Thoreau said it best – *Heaven is under our feet as well as over our heads*. We have to slow down and breathe.

I took stock and gave thanks for the blessings of having a roof over my head, food on my table, bills to pay (which meant my needs were met), hot water for a shower, electricity to keep me warm or cool, devoted caregivers for my autistic son, and the love-of-my-life dog, my best friend and constant companion, Zen.

Recognizing the blessing of the friends in my life who loved and supported me made the days and months in quarantine easier to bear. However, don't think for a minute that I didn't have moments of feeling the most alone I've ever felt. I did. Being singular rather than plural through a trying time like this was a challenge for many of us. But I know this dystopian-looking world we now inhabit isn't our final destination, so I work to focus on the fact that we're just passing through. Five years ago, if anyone of us were asked where we saw ourselves five years into the future, not one of us would have answered with the reality of 2020. Seemingly our world was falling apart, but the prophetic timeline makes it clear that the opposite is true - everything is falling into place. That should give us hope in these uncertain times and that hope should be the reason we keep looking up!

Dreama Denver *was married for three decades to TV icon Bob Denver, known to millions worldwide as the star of the television classic Gilligan's Island. The two met when they were cast opposite one another in a theater production, and toured the country for many years performing together. An author and speaker, Dreama keeps Bob's legacy alive via her work with The Denver Foundation, supporting special needs children and U.S. veterans. Dreama Denver is a Zoom Into Books Author.*

My COVID-19 Experience

by Sabrina Runyon, Ed.D.

March 12, 2020, I, along with hundreds of WV educators, made our way to hotels in Roanoke, WV, in anticipation of attending the WV Mathematics Conference at Stonewall Jackson Resort.

The next morning, I received a call from my assistant superintendent, informing me that Mingo County was canceling schools because of flooding and road issues. Several calls later, I was told that schools would be canceled due to COVID until further notice. I was running late, but I didn't want the teachers from my county to worry, so I was speeding. I did get stopped by a nice police officer who asked where I was going. After telling him the situation, he said that I had too much to worry about besides getting a ticket, so he issued me a warning. When I got to the conference, people were already leaving, afraid of the virus. Most of the attendees stayed and participated in the conference, both days.

The situation worsened. Teachers across the nation were asked to do online teaching. It was a difficult time for students, parents, and educators. Our county was at a disadvantage because our staff was not in their buildings to make plans or get supplies because of the school closing. The governor made a declaration that schools would feed the students throughout the remainder of the year and summer. I helped pack up food and rode a school bus to help deliver the meals. This was rewarding.

People went crazy, buying up all the toilet paper, Clorox wipes, baby wipes and diapers, water, masks, gloves, and groceries. Fortunately, I had ordered toilet paper, laundry detergent, dryer sheets, Kleenex tissues, and paper towels and had them delivered from a specialty store. Stores began limiting items to one or two per customer. Deep freezers were bought by people who had bought all the meats and other freezer items.

The news was scary, showing videos and pictures of entire hospital floors of patients with COVID and stores with empty shelves. The death toll kept rising. Some states went into lockdown, not allowing people out of their homes.

There were inspiring pictures and videos of neighbors helping those who needed help. The frontline workers at hospitals were getting positive attention, with businesses offering free food and products to them.

Ironically, I was supposed to be a part of an educator team that was supposed to travel to China for ten days in April. This was canceled, very quickly, when the news of COVID-19 hit. I had completed my paperwork, had my passport ready, and was so excited. I was so disappointed not to get to go.

My husband and I had bought a new home in December, so COVID allowed me to be at home for a while to paint and do some decorating. I had to order most of the furniture online, so I did a lot of furniture assembling.

Most places were shut down—restaurants, fast-food places, large and small businesses, beauty salons, and doctor's offices. After a while, many places began doing virtual meetings, including doctors.

My husband was allowed to stay home for four days, but had to return to his office. My older son, an essential worker, worked every day. His wife, a beautician, had to stop doing hair, but her online business flourished. My younger son was off work for two weeks, but then had to return. His wife, a nurse, worked every day.

The hardest part of COVID was not being around my family and going to church. I stayed away from everyone except my younger son and his family. I babysat my youngest granddaughter a few days per week.

After a couple of weeks into the pandemic, I was involved in online team meetings for the WVDE, our district office, and our collaborative partners. Some days were spent sitting at my dining room table, on a computer, for many hours. For some of those meetings, my younger granddaughter was on my lap. The central office staff went in at odd times to get some things accomplished, but not everyone came on the same days. At this point, we were already working on a re-entry plan for the upcoming school term.

My older granddaughter turned 1-year-old on March 21st, but we didn't get to see her. My son did a Facetime call so we could see her with her presents. My younger granddaughter turned one-year-old on April 7th, so her parents brought her to our home to do a Facebook Live video of her as she opened her gifts.

Easter was sad—no church services, no grandchildren hunting eggs at our house. We did get to see our oldest grandchildren from their porch, through a glass door, for the first time in a month. My husband and I both were teary-eyed as we drove away.

Churches around the country were closed, but many began doing online services. Some churches had "drive-in" church. Our church did this for a few weeks. It was wonderful to see the other church members, even from a distance. My dad, sister, brother, and sister-in-law attend my church, so I got to see them.

Many incentives were given to people. A stimulus check per family member was sent to people who qualified, each student was given money on a card to help with purchasing food, and our state school system continued to feed the students. People on unemployment were given an extra $600 per week.

My dad, siblings, and nephews built my dad a house during this time. They were together throughout the entire pandemic. I was not involved because I wanted to continue to watch my granddaughter. I felt guilty, but I wouldn't risk getting exposed to the virus.

When the number of cases began decreasing in our area, certain businesses were allowed to reopen, with restrictions.

The beauty shops opened back up. This was a good thing because everyone who has to dye their hair was looking pretty rough—including me. I had to text my daughter-in-law when I arrived at the shop, and everyone had to wear a mask. They cleaned everything, every time someone touched something.

Other stores began opening. There were lines of people waiting to get into the stores. The stores could only have 50% capacity. Although businesses had signs that masks were required, so many didn't abide by the rule.

Organizations had to cancel conferences, conventions, proms, graduations, etc. I was supposed to have been in Texas for two weeks in June for the National Beta Club convention. As a board member, our organization decided to hold a virtual convention. I was supposed to be in Florida for a few days for a Model Schools Conference at the end of June. The conference was held virtually, also. Not getting to travel to these events was very disappointing.

Just like many people, staying home, I was gaining some weight. On May 7th, I began a new health journey. It has expanded into my becoming a certified health coach with the company. It has changed my life. I am smaller than I have been in years, and I hope to decrease my medications.

May 10, 2020, Mother's Day was so special. I came home from "drive-in" church and all my children and grandchildren were there. My oldest granddaughter ran to me with her little arms open, and I almost cried. Getting hugs from her and my grandson was priceless. They had surprised me with dinner and cake. We enjoyed being together for the first time in a long time, and I didn't want that day to end.

Our district office required central office staff to report back on June 3, 2020. Some people chose to wear a mask; others didn't. Many meetings took place, trying to figure out the best way to educate our students. First-grade through twelfth-grade students have one-to-one devices and PK and Kindergarten students will also have them.

By the time Father's Day came around, people were feeling confident that the worst of the virus was over. I had a cookout at my house. Some chose to attend, and some didn't, depending on their comfort level. People began going out of state for vacations and having large gatherings.

The confidence ended when the numbers of cases in WV began rising significantly. The governor declared that gatherings were going back to a limit of 25, and people were to wear masks when inside public places.

So here we are on July 22, 2020, with more new cases being reported than ever before in our community. What happens next is anyone's guess. All I can do is wear my mask, follow the safety guidelines, pray for those who are, or will be affected by COVID-19.

Dr. Sabrina Runyon *has been an educator for 30 years. She is married with two sons. Dr. Runyon finished her doctoral studies in 2016 from Phoenix University. Her first book,* Sabrina's Book, *is a multi-award winning book and came about as an introductory poem to her fellow doctoral classmates in her first year of residency. The sequel,* Kindergarten Kapers, *was released in 2020. Sabrina Runyon is a Zoom Into Books Author.*

Student Authors

The following sixth grade students attend Central Preston Middle School in West Virginia. Their essays are part of a summer Social Studies assignment about how the students were living history at this moment in their lives and asked how would they tell their story.

Rilee Ruggles

My life in quarantine was kind of, well, awful but also good in a way. It was awful because the last day we were in school, but we didn't know it, was the Saint Patrick day dance. We were doing our work in Social Studies when all of a sudden, the monitor started speaking.

"May I have your attention, please?" Our social studies teacher Mrs. Shubert quieted us all down. "Due to COVID-19, all after-school activities will be canceled from today and on out until further notice." Or something like that, but then everyone started talking.

They were saying things like, "That means the dance is canceled!"

"So, I guess I won't be playing basketball now!" And while everyone else was talking, I was wondering, *How will we do classes if we can't be in school?*

Well, this is how. We have been using Microsoft teams to video chat, do schoolwork, and even just talk to each other. Even outside of school, things were canceled. I was going to try out for soccer, but it was canceled. Some stores were closed; many people could not work or earn money, which meant it would be hard for them and even so many more families to buy food and other needs. Governor Jim Justice has started to reopen activities and places again (around April 2020).

But there are a few bright sides to this pandemic. While I'm doing schoolwork, I can eat whatever I want, when I want! And I get to spend more time with my family. And relax more. Plus, it's almost summer vacation, so I am very excited! And just remember reader, we will overcome this, and if it happens to you, just do what we did.

WASH YOUR HANDS.

STAY SIX FEET APART FROM ONE ANOTHER.

WEAR A FACE MASK.

IF YOU THINK YOU HAVE SYMPTOMS GO TO THE HOSPITAL!

DONT STAY IN LARGE GROUPS OF PEOPLE.

And don't go crazy over toilet paper like we did okay?

Colson Manko

It was a regular Friday in March when we got the news that school would be out for a while. Some teachers said it would be one week, two weeks, and some said even more, but it turned out we would not return to school. I was very upset when I found out the news because I did not get to say goodbye to my friends and teachers. I can still remember sitting in English class and someone saying that this could be our last day of school. Our teacher said, "Don't say that. You'll make me start crying." Then, we learned that we would be continuing school online.

We started online schooling on the 19th of March. School online was a lot like what we would do if we were in the building because we have a lot of classes that we use our computers almost every day. I would start my school online about 8:00, and finish about 9:30 or 10:00 depending on what I got finished the day before. Some of my classes had two-day assignments, but I worked hard and finished them the day they were assigned. One day, I might have a hard day, and the next, I would have a very easy day. It just depended on what we were doing in that certain class.

Next, my family and I have been spending a lot of time together. Since all the sports were canceled, our weeknights are not jam-packed with sports every night. We have been spending more family time in our living room. My mom is the Director of Nursing at Pine Ridge in Kingwood, WV. When she comes home, she goes straight to the shower and changes her clothes. My mom says she is on two to three calls a day about Covid-19. Luckily, when Governor Justice had all the nursing homes tested, there were no positive tests at the nursing home where she works. My mom didn't know what she would do if they had a positive case, and she even talked about not coming home if they had a positive case.

So, you may wonder - while my mom was at work, what do I do? I have been waking up about 9:00, and I play Hay Day on my phone or look on social media until about 9:45. Then I get out of bed, and I go take care of my chickens and ducks with my sister. My big chickens' names are Annie, Socks, Boxer, Tiny, Cliff, and Hatcher. I get about 3 or 4 eggs a day from them. I have six baby chicks named Flash, Willow, Lucy, Lucky, Bo, and Vanilla. They all are four weeks old. I clean their water bucket out every day. Then my ducks' names are K and Elly. They are so big, and they are also four weeks old. They have a small pool in their pen that they like to go in, and they must think it is a toilet. As soon as I clean it out, they go in it. My older chickens and ducks hang out in the pen during the day together.

Then I come up to my house and I read my book *Harry Potter and the Prisoner of Azkaban*, or I jump on my trampoline that I got for Easter. I am about halfway through my book, and I love it. On my trampoline, my sister Ryelyn and I play a game with small rubber basketballs where you jump around and try not to get hit. Also, one day a week, I must mow the bottom half of my yard. Then I go out to my grandparents to help my grandma mow and weed eat. I haven't seen my grandma as much as I would like to right now, but we try to Facetime at least every day or every other day. We talk for about thirty minutes. We talk about all kinds of stuff like what we are watching on Netflix or TV and what everyone else is doing. For example, my grandad and my grandma always ask about my siblings.

My Nana just opened her pool, and my sister and I go up every other night and swim for about two hours. Most of the time, you can find me in my room, watching my favorite TV series, "Once Upon A Time." It is about Emma Swan who must go to StoryBrooke to break a curse that Regina Mills, AKA the Evil Queen, has cast. There are seven seasons and one hundred fifty-six episodes. Even though I enjoy doing all these things, I missed a lot from the end of school.

On the 15th of March, they announced that my Flex class had won the food drive, and we were supposed to have a trip to Dairy Queen, but it didn't happen. We also were having a dance that night that I was supposed to help at the photo booth, but the dance was canceled. The one thing I was mainly sad about was not getting to have the house party. I felt we had a fantastic chance this year of taking the cup, but I feel just as good this coming year. As everyone knows, Hephaestus is the Bestus. I also missed the National Junior Honor Society election and induction. The election would have put six new people as officers. The induction would have put this coming 7th graders in the National Junior Honor Society.

As I mentioned before, I was very upset when I could not say goodbye to my friends and teachers. The end of the year awards are always my favorite, and this year I worked hard to try to get the most AR points in this year's 7th grade, and I was really upset when I did not find out if I had the most points or who had the most points. Also, there were no end of the year trips, so I did not go to Big Bear to play a "clean" game of basketball with Mrs. Shubert and a few other people. Also, I was excited to play mini-golf with Head Band and Queen, hopefully. As you can see, I missed out on a lot of things in just a couple of months.

My life, since this has started, has calmed down like a lot of other peoples. My family and I have grown closer, and we are moving faster in our addition to our house. Almost every night, we can sit down together as a family and have a meal because before there would be some type of sports event every single night. We can also have nice, calm weekends having fun and riding as a family. No one at my house watches the news really except my dad. My oldest sister usually has dinner ready about 5. My dad is home about four or a little after and my mom gets home about five or five-thirty.

I have heard so many rumors about what school will be like next year. I hope that I can be back in the classroom because that is where I do my best learning. There were times this year during online schooling when I thought if I was in class, then I would walk up there and ask a question if I needed help. I like hands-on learning and watching the teacher demonstrate it. Also, I missed having friends there to help you out, and to talk to about what you get and don't get is a blessing in disguise. I loved being able to laugh and joke with my friends all year long.

And on the 21st of May, year 2020, I, Colson Manko, 13 of Albright officially became an 8th grader at Central Preston Middle School.

Dayton Wilson

During March 2020, a virus called the Coronavirus or Covid-19 began spreading across the United States. The first states that it began affecting were California and Washington. West Virginia was one of the last states to become affected by the Coronavirus. On March 13, the Governor of West Virginia announced that at the end of the school day, schools were going to close indefinitely. Our lives changed big time. After that, the governor announced a "Stay at Home Order" for the state of West Virginia. Other states had already gotten to this point and were living like this, but now it had come to WV. Now the only going out of the house that would be done would be for emergencies or to get necessities. Everyone was experiencing mass chaos.

If you go to the store, the store shelves are practically bare. Things have been picked over and there is hardly anything to choose from. Also, toilet paper and paper towels are nowhere to be found. People have begun hoarding toilet paper, paper towels, Lysol wipes, and cleaners. It is hard to shop for things you need when the stores are wiped out. There has also been the initiation of wearing masks and gloves whenever you are out anywhere. Stores have now limited the number of people that can be shopping in the store at one time. They also have directional arrows on the floor to show you which way to go, so that it limits contact with people. There is also a six-foot apart rule to follow for social distancing.

All these changes are almost too much to handle. People are panicking and stressed about everything. Restaurants, gyms, salons, barbershops, malls, stores, etc. are all closed due to the Covid 19. Other things that were canceled were NBA, XFL, NASCAR races, hockey, local sports, including spring soccer that I play, baseball, tee-ball, and more. The only places open are essential businesses and the only people working are essential workers. Now with people not working and laid off, paying bills has become an issue. The government is working toward getting all Americans money, but it is a work in progress.

All schools have gone to online learning and teachers are

working very hard to provide work for the students to continue their education and learning at home. The only problem with that is that some students do not have the ability to have internet, so this is a problem when it comes to doing their online schoolwork. Teachers are working to provide paper packets for students as well. All of this is brand new to everyone. It is taking a toll on everyone in several ways. Every day I had homework in Science, Social Studies, English, Flex, and Math. There were times that I had work to do in Gym. All of this was just different. Not being in school with the teachers puts all the work and learning on the student and parents are trying to help out. I did adjust to the new online learning system after about a month, but I would have rather been back in school. Each day I had to finish my schoolwork and do chores around the house. After that, I would play my game systems, shoot basketball, ride my four-wheeler, or play with the animals. We hardly went anywhere. My parents would go to the store to get essentials, but I would stay home. We did go fishing a few times, just our family to a pond where nobody else was fishing. We also took some hikes through the woods and on the rail trails. I kept hoping things would go back to normal, but a month went by and no change. Then Governors everywhere were announcing that schools would not be back in session this academic year. I was keeping my fingers crossed that WV would not join this situation. However, next came the announcement from the Governor of WV that schools would remain closed for this school year. Bummed and disgusted is how I felt. Everything was different now and we could not even go to school for the rest of the year. However, we did have to continue our online learning every day. So, the only thing to do was try to adjust to the "new" normal.

I feel bad for the students that are Seniors this year because they are missing a lot. They canceled prom, graduation, etc. These students are finishing up their last year in school and cannot experience any of the things that they should be experiencing. They are closing a chapter in their life under this Covid 19 situation. Also, I feel bad for the 8th graders. My sister is in 8th grade and she is missing out on so many things that happen during the 8th

grade year. She missed her spring formal, pictures, 8th grade evening, graduation from middle school and more. She will go to high school next year, so this was a big year for her.

I will always remember 2020 as the year everyone hoarded toilet paper, you had to stay at home, and we couldn't go to school. This is going to be a time to remember as everything changed for everyone. I had to adjust to the "new" normal just like everyone else, but it did not make things less hard. The only good thing out of this whole situation was it gave people time to slow down and families come together and have more family time. Not having to rush to practices and games gave our family more time together to do things; however, we had to stay at home or practice social distancing with what we did.

Tyler Cole

I never thought going to school on Friday, March 13, 2020, as being the last day I would actually be in school for my sixth-grade year. We were placed in quarantine starting on Monday and doing virtual school the remainder of the school term on May 21. It was a little scary as businesses and restaurants began closing or placing very strict precautions on entering. It was very strange to be at home and still doing schoolwork, just like normal. The teachers had to provide a whole new way of instruction online.

I was home the first week and then my mom's business made them work from home, so that was cool because we got to spend a lot of time together. I played Fortnite and Minecraft with some of my friends from school during this time. It was difficult to find some items at the store because people went crazy on bought a bunch of things they really did not need. We never did without anything that we had to have; it seemed like it was always provided. I never worried about getting the virus. I did worry about my grandparents, though. They were older and may not have been able to recover. Churches were even closed, but that did not stop the preachers. Several of them started doing live streaming on Facebook to keep in touch with the people.

We were told that the Coronavirus started in China. All travel was stopped, and it became hard for stores to get supplies delivered due to the virus. This did not affect me any because we didn't have to travel.

I am glad most people listened and stayed home as much as possible to help get the Coronavirus under control. It seemed like it was a long time to be in quarantine, but it really wasn't. Some counties had to cancel their fairs and public pools were closed for the summer of 2020. I am very glad that all my family and friends remained safe and well through all the pandemic.

Lilly Moats

For me, my advice is to be prepared to stock up on things such as toilet paper, soap, hand sanitizer, things to keep clean, and things that you are going to need. For me, the quarantine has not been so bad, but it is not fun either because we can't really go out and do stuff. We cannot go into restaurants and stuff like that, but other than that, quarantine has not been that bad. I miss all my friends and teachers!

My life did not change much other than having to be stuck at home all the time, not being able to see people, and not being able to go in the stores. Quarantine was also a good thing because it gave me time to myself and let me get some exercise. I could play outside more and did not have to do a bunch of schoolwork as usual. But I would not want to do online schooling after quarantine because I honestly do not like online school.

When they told us school is shutting down, I was shocked. I knew there was a coronavirus, but I did not think it was that bad. We were had told that there was a dance at school, and they had to cancel it. I remember going into Walmart with my parents and family that day so we could get food and we went over to see if we could get some toilet paper and not one package of toilet paper was on a shelf!

At first, when I heard of coronavirus, I did not think it was going to be so bad. I thought it was just going to be like a little cold or something, but I found out that the virus was way worse than I thought. Honestly, I will never forget the coronavirus just because we have been quarantined so long and that is never really happened before. It is a period in your life you are not going to forget. How I kept busy was to play outside and spend time with family watching TV, playing with my animals, and just the normal stuff that I would do.

Bella Miller

It all started on March 13; all the county schools shut their doors, not knowing it would be the last day of normal. Quarantine just began. We had online schooling instead of waking up early and going to school. To help people not be bored at this time, people started spring cleaning early, daily walks to get fresh air, and watching every episode of Tiger King. My old life was now a thing in the past. Now everywhere we go, it is more common to wear a face mask, be six feet apart, and be more cautious of the germs out there. One memory I will remember is that to keep from being bored, we cleaned every single room into the house and did lots of yard work.

The quarantine did bring some good to me because we got to spend more time as a family and do things we would not do regularly. If another disease came or something else pops up and we need to be in quarantine, I would give the advice that things will get better and look on the brighter side. In other countries, people do not have a house they can stay in.

The one thing that I did not think I would miss is school. After doing online schooling for about three months, I want to go back and see my future teachers and past teachers and, of course, my friends. I will not take school or even going to the store for granted after quarantine.

Garrett Haymond

Humans need many things to live — food, water, and human interaction, just to name a few. Early in 2020 year we got a new pandemic called COVID-19 (Coronavirus) and had to self-quarantine, which meant we would have to stay home and do school instead of going to school. I will remember this quarantine by three categories -Schools have been shut down and everything with it, the interactions with friends are ruined, and The Good and Bad of Self- Quarantine.

In early March of 2020, the West Virginia governor issued a stay at home order that required everything to shut down until further notice. Then a few days after schools have been shut down, we started online school which from writing this we are still on that online format. When the government issued the stay at home order, stores were hit and started to go out of business, and massive amounts of people were laid off. As I write this, 30 million have filed for unemployment. If you are a sports fanatic, this is not the year for you, because some of the events people were waiting for have beenshut down (March Madness and Olympics). But a least we got the Super Bowl.

It is May 19, 2020, and summertime is around the corner, and when that time comes around, people get excited about certain things. For me, the things I get excited is Baseball season, Summer Camp, and seeing my friends. Baseball season is cut into two times of the year Spring Ball (which is more competitive) and Fall Ball (Basically Practice season), but as of a few days ago, baseball was canceled. Summer camp usually starts in mid-June to July and can be fun because we go on field trips and go to the pool every week. However, if quarantine is still here then I won't be able to see anyone there or go to the pool, but I'm pretty sure if it's still here, I'm just going to swim at my friend's house.

Every year there are good things that happen and bad things that happen. In this quarantine, we have seen many good things that gave the famed actor John Krasinski the idea to start a show called SGN (Some Good News), which captured the good things of quarantine. We also got Tiger King, which was about the story of Joe Exotic. 2020 can be divided into Good and Bad, 2020 had a rough start from the Australian bush fires and Kobe Bryant's death, and that was just in January. February saw the Super Bowl, World War lll scares, and the first American death by Corona.

In conclusion, the world will never be the same after this quarantine. In my opinion, this is just the first of many, so buckle your seat belt because this is going to be a bumpy six months.

Jillian Conn

This is how I would tell my coronavirus pandemic story—living in history. When the virus first started, it was a rumor that this man had gotten a virus from eating a bat in China. Nobody would think that the virus would spread anywhere else. Here we are with the USA with the most cases! The stores were jam-packed with people buying food, toilet paper, and cleaning supplies so much that there had to be a limit of just 1 or 2. Some of the shelves were completely empty. On Tuesdays, at Kingwood Walmart, the elderly are allowed to shop in the morning, so they don't get sick. In the future, there is supposed to be another wave of coronavirus.

What I did to keep busy in this historical time was go outside and play basketball and throw the softball, I did a bunch of puzzles and board games, and I did a bunch of crafts. My life changed because we couldn't go to school and I couldn't see my friends and family, and we had to wear masks when we went out, and we had to put on hand sanitizer when we came out of stores. We only thought this virus would only last a month, but then it canceled the rest of the school year, which meant no more school activities. We just had to keep listening to the governor and what his state rules where. We also had to stay 6 feet apart from people that are not the people we live with. I also could not play sports. We also had to order to go instead of going inside restaurants and eating! All the stores and buildings were shutting down too!

I will remember the pandemic by making more memories with my family. Good things came with quarantine because I got to hang out with my family more! (Well obviously the ones I live with!) I felt a little upset because I didn't get to finish my last year of grasshopper basketball, but I was also afraid because my dad has to go to work because he is the manager of Walmart, and a bunch of people go to his store. I think that this virus is crazy, but if we stick together, we will hopefully get through it, but if people do not stay home and hang out with their friends, it's not going to stop spreading.

I would say always wear a mask and try and stay home, stock up on food, stay 6 feet apart, call your loved ones and your elders and ask if they need anything from the store. When you get home from going anywhere, use Lysol to spray yourself down or come inside and get a shower right away to get any germs off your body. Always have hand sanitizer and cleaning products to clean all surfaces to get all the germs away!

The New Normal

by Don Helin

March 2020. The sun shone brightly when I pulled into my dry cleaners to drop off shirts. The winter months had been kind to us in central Pennsylvania and we were hoping spring would be the same.

I stepped out of my Toyota Highlander and opened the door. Penny looked up from behind the counter. "Hey, Don, got a couple of shirts to drop off?"

"Yep. Need them back by the weekend. Off to Houston next Tuesday for the Texas Library Association Conference."

"Sounds like fun. They'll be ready Friday. What do you think of this virus?"

"Scares me. The first virus cases in the U.S. hit Washington state in January and it's spreading like mad. Not sure what it all means."

Penny filled out a form for the shirts. "Bad in other countries, too. I heard on the news it's a global pandemic."

I took the form and slipped it into my billfold. "See you in a couple of days. Stay well."

Little things come along and you don't realize their impact until later — much later. It would be months before I would pull that form out of my billfold again.

That evening, I turned the news on to hear our governor order a statewide shutdown of all non-life sustaining businesses with enforcement going into effect in Pennsylvania on March 27th.

I looked at my wife. "What does it mean?"

"I don't know, but it sounds bad."

The governor talked about health concerns from COVID-19, as well as the stock market crash. I watched with trepidation the fall of several percentage points in the world's major indices over the next few days, wondering what it meant for my own stocks.

Things changed quickly. Instead of thinking about the appointments I had, where we would eat tonight, how long would it take us to drive to our friend's house, my new mantra became—wear your mask, wash your hands, and stay home.

I worried about our family — two daughters and a son in Texas and a daughter in nearby Malvern. And grandchildren. Would they be careful? News broadcasts parroted the terror from the virus moving across the country and the world.

I remembered New Year's Eve. The excitement I had felt for the upcoming year. Trips for signings and workshops, visits to family, and two high school graduations — our granddaughter close by in Malvern and our grandson in San Antonio.

Within two weeks, all these plans came crashing down around me. Schools and businesses closed, workshops canceled, and the governor's stay at home order made it clear no one was going anywhere.

The simple task of going to stores became dangerous, so different than only a month before. "Do we dare go?" I asked my wife.

"We need food. Wear your mask."

"Okay. Quick in and out. Masks, social distancing, hand washing. Will that be enough to protect us?"

"Has to be."

Scared me. What if it wasn't?

We stayed home. A complete change in the way we shopped, exercised, ate, sought entertainment. I didn't like it, but couldn't do a darn thing about it.

I thought about small business owners and workers losing not only their jobs, but their livelihood — maybe their homes. The economy evolved into a desperate condition. Would we be in economic trouble, too?

We lived in an over-55 retirement community and had many friends — enjoyed playing cards and other games as well as going out to shows and sharing meals.

In our community, I knew friends who had lost their partners and lived alone. In order to keep social distance, the culinary staff delivered meals to rooms rather than serving people in the dining room.

Residents would eat alone in their room day after day, night after night, keeping them safe from this highly contagious virus. But, these people didn't see family, friends, only a staff person once in a while.

I passed an elderly friend in the hallway. "How are you doing?"

She started to cry. "If this is all there is to my life anymore, I don't want to wake up in the morning."

What could I say? Couldn't touch her — hug her, take her hand.

"I am so sorry." I watch her walk down the hall.

People across the country were dying in huge numbers. School closures, job disruptions, and the threat to the elderly and low-income families were only a few aspects of this evolving crisis. I stood by helpless—nothing I could do.

In-person graduation ceremonies for our granddaughter and grandson were canceled—just one of many hits we had to swallow.

Over the next thirteen weeks, Lancaster County would report almost 4,000 confirmed cases, and sadly 329 deaths. Many of those who died, passed away without family or friends by their side due to isolation. I realized we would never return to normal, but rather some sort of new normal. I could only guess what it might look like

---

The governor spoke on television in early May. "The mitigation efforts have helped curtail the spread of COVID-19," he said. "The key for us now must be that hospitals can continue to treat patients without overwhelming their limited supplies of personal protective equipment (PPE), ventilators, or beds."

As our situation stabilized, his administration planned a measured approach, allowing Pennsylvanians to return to work safely without a spike in the number of new cases. This method had to balance the return to economic stability, while at the same time caring for people's health.

The most restrictive red phase had the sole purpose of minimizing the spread of COVID-19 through strict social distancing, closing of all non-life sustaining businesses, and mandatory stay at home orders. We feared this would last until scientists found a vaccine.

A goal for reopening was initially set at having fewer than 50 new confirmed cases per 100,000 population over the previous 14 days. Other factors included sufficient testing available, a contact-tracing capability, and hospitals having sufficient staff and equipment available for new patients.

As Pennsylvania moved through the three phases from red to yellow to green, I watched the political pressure mount for the governor to speed the process. I hated the fighting and negative tenor of the discussion, people yelling at one another. People were dying, sinking into depression. It seemed to me the last thing we needed was fighting. Sadly it continued.

Our county moved from red to yellow in early June, which meant businesses such as retailers could operate with 50% occupancy, increasing to 75 % in Green. Gatherings had to be less than 25 people in yellow, but could increase to 250 in green.

In the yellow phase, restaurants and bars were limited to carry out and eating outside, while in green, table service inside could be provided for customers up to 50% occupancy. Who would measure this? Would it still be fun to eat out?

Was this to be the new normal? As we traveled around the county, I saw people breaking the rules — not wearing masks, not social distancing, gathering in large groups — leading to spikes in cases of the virus. How could they do this? People were dying.

WHAT DID I LEARN?

Treasure every moment. I took for granted the opportunity to spend time with friends, go to movies and plays. The virus had destroyed every piece of that.

Know your enemy. The virus is neither good nor evil, but the effect is overwhelming. I learned exactly how the virus spreads from one person to another and worked hard to manage our risk.

Don't go into crowded places. Wear a mask. Social Distance. By managing risk, we could do many of the things we wanted while staying safe. We still were limited on close family visits, but going on bike rides together, eating outside on a porch, and social distancing from others worked. At least so far.

A few days ago, I walked into my dry cleaners. Penny stood behind the counter.

When she saw me, she called through her mask, "Welcome back, Don. Don't you have some shirts here?"

I pulled the form out of my billfold, unfolded the crumpled paper, and handed it to her. "I can't tell you how good it is to see you. Wasn't sure I ever would again."

During his time in the military, **Don Helin** *served at a number of stateside posts as well as overseas in Vietnam and Germany. He is the author of six thrillers that draw from his military experience, including three tours in the Pentagon. He writes for* TheBurg, *a community magazine based in Harrisburg.*

Don's novel, Secret Assault, *was selected as the Best Suspense/Thriller at the 2015 Indie Book Awards and* Long Walk Home *won a Five Star review at the Readers Favorite Awards. His novel,* Roof of the World, *recently was honored as a Finalist in the 2020 Indie Book Awards. Don Helin is a Zoom Into Books Author.*

Acknowledgments

Many thanks to all who contributed to this memoir collection, without them there would be no book. I especially want to thank Don Helin for his excellent writing workshops on Zoom Into Books and his collaboration and editing on this book. Thank you to Ellen Shubert and her students from Central Preston Middle School for their contributions to this unique edition.

Thank you to my sister, Patti Wood, and the South Carolina support team: Toni McCammon, Fran Watson, Barbara McGill, Randi Cramer, Bee Baldassano—all excellent critics and advisors.

Much gratitude and thanks to my talented daughter, Ashley Belote, for her expert design skills and her husband, Scott Belote, for all the heavy lifting and his excellent tech skills. He is the reason I remain online and functional.

Covid-19 has made its mark on all of us and this is one of the most bizarre times in history that we will never forget. It has made all of us reinvent ourselves, brought blessings and curses, but most of all, given us all time to reflect on our lives, our country, and our faith.

Cathy Teets
President, Headline Books Inc